Enhancing the Contribution of Sport to the Sustainable Development Goals

Iain Lindsey and Tony Chapman

Commonwealth Secretariat
Marlborough House
Pall Mall
London
SW1Y 5HX
United Kingdom

Published by the Commonwealth Secretariat
Authored by Iain Lindsey and Tony Chapman (Durham University)
Additional research by Sarah Metcalfe (Durham University)
Project initiated and managed by Oliver Dudfield and Malcolm Dingwall-Smith (Commonwealth Secretariat)
Edited by Prepress Projects Limited
Typeset by NovaTechset Private Limited, Bengaluru & Chennai, India
Cover design by Commonwealth Secretariat
Printed and bound by CPI Group (UK) Ltd, Croydon, CR0 4YY

Copies of this publication may be obtained from

Publications Section
Commonwealth Secretariat
Marlborough House
Pall Mall
London
SW1Y 5HX
United Kingdom
Tel: +44 (0)20 7747 6534
Fax: +44 (0)20 7839 9081
Email: publications@commonwealth.int
Web: www.thecommonwealth.org/publications

A catalogue record for this publication is available from the British Library.

ISBN (paperback): 978-1-84929-165-1
ISBN (e-book): 978-1-84859-959-8

Contents

List of figures

List of tables

List of boxes

Abbreviations and acronyms

CABOS	Commonwealth Advisory Body on Sport
CGF	Commonwealth Games Federation
GDP	Gross domestic product
ILO	International Labour Organization
IOC	International Olympic Committee
MDG	Millennium Development Goal
NGO	Non-governmental organisation
SDG	Sustainable Development Goal
UNCTAD	United Nations Conference on Trade and Development
UNESCO	United Nations Education, Scientific and Cultural Organization
UNICEF	United Nations International Children's Emergency Fund
WHO	World Health Organization

Executive summary

The *2030 Agenda for Sustainable Development,* adopted by the United Nations General Assembly in September 2015, sets out a 'supremely ambitious and transformational vision' for global development (UNGA 2015, para. 7, 3). The 17 Sustainable Development Goals (SDGs) and their associated targets are comprehensive and far-reaching in scope and 'balance the three dimensions of sustainable development: the economic, social and environmental' (UNGA 2015, preamble, 1).

The 'growing contribution of sport to the realization of development and peace' (UNGA 2015, para. 37, 10) is explicitly identified in the 2030 Agenda for Sustainable Development.

The 'growing contribution of sport to the realization of development and peace' (UNGA 2015, para. 37, 10) is explicitly identified in the *2030 Agenda for Sustainable Development.* The statement represents an important milestone for sport and an opportunity to build on previous commitments and progress made by the Commonwealth, the United Nations and other international, national and local stakeholders. This guide supports this endeavour through providing direction for governmental policy-makers, and other stakeholders, to enable sport to make the fullest possible contribution to sustainable development.

Previous Commonwealth publications have presented analysis (Commonwealth Secretariat 2016) and key principles (Kay and Dudfield 2013) for sport and sustainable development. This guide builds on these publications to recommend evidenced and balanced policy options to support the effective and cost-efficient contribution of sport towards six prioritised SDGs. All identified policy options align with the importance accorded to the 'means of implementation' through SDG 17.

Sustainable Development Goal 3: Ensure healthy lives and promote well-being for all, at all ages

Universal and holistic conceptions of health and well-being are at the forefront of the *2030 Agenda for Sustainable Development.* Linked to SDG target 3.4, evidence strongly shows that regular physical activity reduces the risks of a number of non-communicable diseases and indicates further benefits for psychological and social health. Reducing globally significant levels of physical inactivity among adults and children of both sexes is therefore a priority which can, in part, be addressed through efforts to increase participation in sport.

Utilisation of sport as an attractive and flexible context for health education and empowerment can also contribute to SDG targets 3.3, 3.5 and 3.7, which address various communicable diseases, substance abuse, and sexual and reproductive health, respectively.

A number of benefits of alignment between policies that span sport, physical activity and public health can be identified. Resources can be levered and targeted from a number of different sources, and their use may balance the prioritisation of infrastructure that can support population-level change with scaling-up of targeted initiatives that have proved effective. Complementary approaches can benefit from the expertise of sport- and health-based practitioners, who can also benefit from mutual capacity-building. Utilising standardised measures of sport participation and physical activity within data collection systems for health and in specific sport-based initiatives can also enhance evidence-based policy-making.

A number of benefits of alignment between policies that span sport, physical activity and public health can be identified.

Sustainable Development Goal 4: Ensure inclusive and equitable quality education and promote lifelong learning opportunities for all

Established by international declarations as a 'fundamental right for all' (UNESCO 2013a, b, 2015), physical education, physical activity and sport represent an important component of, and contributor to, holistic education. High-quality physical education and sport can contribute to SDG target 4.1 through enhancing lifelong physical literacy and supporting a range of wider educational benefits.

Physical education, physical activity and sport represent an important component of, and contributor to, holistic education.

Integrating opportunities for experiential learning and youth leadership into sport-based activities can also contribute to SDG targets 4.4 and 4.7 which focus on wider personal, skill and knowledge development. SDG target 4.5 signals the need to address longstanding inequalities in access to physical education and school-based sport. Positively, sport-based approaches can also be attractive in re-engaging some young people with formal and non-formal education.

While physical education has been declared compulsory in 97 per cent of countries (UNESCO 2013a, b), there is a need for impetus and resources to address significant variations in provision. Training for generalist and specialist teachers, and for adults and young people delivering sport-based activities, can enable the high-quality and inclusive provision that can facilitate diverse educational outcomes. National systems of monitoring and quality assurance can help to prioritise implementation and enable identification of specific areas for improvement.

Sustainable Development Goal 5: Achieve gender equality and empower all women and girls

Gender equality is a cross-cutting issue throughout the *2030 Agenda for Sustainable Development* which has relevance to a number of the SDGs included in this guide. Applying SDG targets 5.1 and 5.5 to sport emphasises the need to address evident gender inequalities at all levels of participation and leadership. Enabling girls' and women's involvement in sport can also serve to challenge broader discriminatory norms and offer specific opportunities for gender empowerment. These contributions of sport to gender equality must further be underpinned by progress towards eliminating all forms of violence and harmful practices against women and girls in sport, in line with SDG targets 5.2 and 5.3.

Policies should ensure the implementation in sport of wider legal frameworks for non-discrimination, seek to embed gender equality across sport and development organisations, and also enable initiatives that can contribute to the empowerment of specific groups of women. Varied opportunities for girls and women's safe involvement in sport are needed to address context-specific needs and barriers, and these can be developed through funding allocations that promote gender equality. Contributions to cultural change, through promoting female role models and involving men and boys in specific initiatives, are also important. Gender disaggregation of all monitoring and evaluation is essential both to prioritise and measure the contribution of sport to gender equality.

Policies should ensure the implementation in sport of wider legal frameworks for non-discrimination, seek to embed gender equality across sport and development organisations, and also enable initiatives that can contribute to the empowerment of specific groups of women.

Sustainable Development Goal 8: Promote sustained, inclusive and sustainable economic growth, full and productive employment and decent work for all

In many countries, the contribution of the sport industry to economic growth and employment is increasingly recognised.

While this contribution is relevant to SDG targets 8.1, 8.5 and 8.9, there are significant complexities in precisely measuring the diverse range of economic and employment activities associated with sport. Therefore, careful analysis should inform decisions to pursue economic impact through sport-event hosting and tourism, and leveraging benefits requires long-term, co-ordinated and context-specific strategies.

Sport-based approaches can engage volunteers and offer specific training to enhance employment prospects, and in so doing contribute to SDG targets 8.5 and 8.6. In line with SDG target 8.3, various models of entrepreneurial practice have also been advanced by sport and development organisations. To increase their effectiveness, all such approaches should be linked to identifiable opportunities for employment and entrepreneurship within sport or other industries.

Sport-based approaches can engage volunteers and offer specific training to enhance employment prospects.

Finally, in respect of SDG targets 8.7 and 8.8, concerns regarding labour rights, abuses in sports manufacturing and construction, and examples of exploitation of young people who are seeking careers in professional sport need to be addressed. While globalisation often provides the context for such problems, national policy-makers are responsible for evidencing and regulating potential abuses, and can promote good employment and developmental practices.

Sustainable Development Goal 11: Make cities and human settlements inclusive, safe, resilient and sustainable

Global trends of urbanisation have significant impacts on various aspects of sustainable development. SDG target 11.7 aligns with UN-Habitat guidance that indicates that a minimum of 15 per cent of urban areas should be allocated for open and green spaces and public facilities (UN Conference on Housing and Sustainable Urban Development 2015). Integrating opportunities for physical activity throughout such spaces and across urban environments can have widespread and long-term impacts.

Integrating opportunities for physical activity throughout such spaces and across urban environments can have widespread and long-term impacts.

Different approaches to integrated design can provide hubs for family- and community-based engagement in various forms of sport and active recreation, and similarly include provision for sport within facilities for education, health and other services. Inclusion, accessibility and safety for all user groups must always be a key design consideration. Designs for sport stadiums can also prioritise reducing environmental impacts, enabling sustainable usage and supporting broader urban regeneration.

SDG target 11.3 draws attention to the importance of inclusive, multi-stakeholder involvement in the planning and management of spaces and facilities. National policy-makers can regulate to preserve green spaces, identify priorities for new developments and specify quality design criteria. Funding for spaces and facilities can be drawn from, and build on, public–private and civil society partnerships. Particularly at local levels, engaging all stakeholder groups from the outset can enhance ongoing management and use of spaces and facilities.

Sustainable Development Goal 16: Promote peaceful and inclusive societies for sustainable development, provide access to justice for all, and build effective, accountable and inclusive institutions at all levels

As is more generally the case, enhancing justice and peace within and through sport is essential to underpin sport-based contributions to other SDGs. Both the high profile of sport and more participatory approaches may be utilised to contribute to the pursuit of peace and reduction of all forms of violence, as prioritised in SDG target 16.1. Sport-based approaches can draw on the cross-cultural status of sport and the work of skilled leaders and appropriate role models, but must also be integrated with wider peace building and violence reduction processes given that conflict and violence have complex and deep-rooted causes.

Both the high profile of sport and more participatory approaches may be utilised to contribute to the pursuit of peace and reduction of all forms of violence.

There is increasing recognition of the need to address multiple challenges to the integrity of sport. Associated with SDG target 16.2, it is vital to combat abuse and all forms of violence against children in sport. Problems of corruption, doping and the manipulation of sporting competition serve to emphasise the need for improvements in governance throughout sport and its institutions, in line with SDG targets 16.5, 16.6 and 16.7.

International standards and recommendations for good governance and child safeguarding in sport are available, but require country-led implementation and can be made a prerequisite for sporting organisations seeking public funds.

Integrated national research and information systems can help to evidence abuse and corruption, monitor organisational compliance and identify examples of best practice for use in capacity-building.

Sustainable Development Goal 17: Strengthen the means of implementation and revitalise the Global Partnership for Sustainable Development

The means of implementation

Realising the scale and ambition of the SDGs requires the means of implementation to be strengthened within each country, and globally. Together, SDG targets 17.14 and 17.15 establish the importance of country-leadership and policy coherence to enhancing collective approaches towards identified SDGs across sectors and among the wide range of sport and development stakeholders. Associated with SDG targets 17.16 and 17.17, further impetus is required to realise the recognised – if unevenly achieved – potential of different forms of partnership in support of the contribution of sport to sustainable development. National policy leadership can also support all organisations to mobilise and direct financial resources and work towards sustainable and scaled capacity-building, in line with SDG targets 17.3 and 17.9.

Aligned with these considerations, relationships between governments and various private and civil society organisations, including sport federations, can be configured in different ways to contribute collectively to sustainable development. Collective implementation can simultaneously encompass approaches that are:

Relationships between governments and various private and civil society organisations, including sport federations, can be configured in different ways to collectively contribute to sustainable development.

- **government led** through the direct provision of services or the regulation of non-governmental stakeholders
- based on **structured partnerships** in which governments work formally with private and civil society organisations to achieve agreed objectives
- supportive of **complementary** relationships of mutual support and/or collaborative delivery involving organisations from different sectors
- receptive to **autonomous** contributions of private and civil society organisations where they are aligned with governmental policy objectives.

Policy options to enhance the contribution of sport to particular SDGs span these different approaches, each of which can work at different scales and require varying governmental capacities and input.

Measuring progress: data, monitoring and accountability

Governments also have responsibility for implementing processes by which progress towards the SDGs are reviewed. This requirement, and the need for capacity-building to meet it, is captured in SDG targets 17.18 and 17.19. In applying these priorities to sport, limitations of the evidence base regarding contributions to development outcomes have been recognised, and emphasis has been placed on improving evaluation of specific sport-based initiatives. Many countries do not, as yet, have national systems of data collection for sport.

Policy-makers can, nevertheless, often draw on and triangulate a range of evidence sources to make reasoned judgements as to the contribution of sport-related policy and interventions towards the SDGs. Different approaches to triangulation are available, and pragmatic methods of identifying the contribution of specific interventions, such as theory-of-change models or social return on investment, have been increasingly used within sport. However, resources and expertise need to be available to enact such methods, and care needs to be taken not to overstate the particular contributions of sport – given the range of other factors beyond sport-based interventions – that can influence progress towards sustainable development.

Concluding implications for policy-makers

In utilising this guide to inform approaches to enhance the contribution of sport to sustainable development, policy-makers are recommended to fully appraise the particular possibilities and constraints for implementation in national and local contexts.

In utilising this guide to inform approaches to enhance the contribution of sport to sustainable development, policy-makers are recommended to appraise fully the particular possibilities and constraints for implementation in national and local contexts. Such an appraisal may consider current levels of development, existing physical, human and organisational infrastructure for sport, and the potential scale and depth of potential sport-based contributions to particular SDGs (see Table ES.1). Strengthening national policy based on such considerations enables appropriately differentiated enactment of policy options for implementation and approaches to measuring progress towards sustainable development.

Table ES.1 The potential contribution of sport-based policy to the global SDG targets

Goal	Target	
3 Good health and well-being	*Direct contribution*	3.4 By 2030, reduce by one-third premature mortality from non-communicable diseases through prevention and treatment and promote mental health and well-being
	Linked contribution	3.3 By 2030, end the epidemics of AIDS, tuberculosis, malaria and neglected tropical diseases and combat hepatitis, water-borne diseases and other communicable diseases 3.5 Strengthen the prevention and treatment of substance abuse, including narcotic drug abuse and harmful use of alcohol 3.7 By 2030, ensure universal access to sexual and reproductive healthcare services, including for family planning, information and education, and the integration of reproductive health into national strategies and programmes
4 Quality education	*Direct Contribution*	4.5 By 2030, eliminate gender disparities in education and ensure equal access to all levels of education and vocational training for the vulnerable, including persons with disabilities, indigenous peoples and children in vulnerable situations
	Linked contribution	4.7 By 2030, ensure that all learners acquire the knowledge and skills needed to promote sustainable development, including through education for sustainable development and sustainable lifestyles, human rights, gender equality, promotion of a culture of peace and non-violence, global citizenship and appreciation of cultural diversity and of culture's contribution to sustainable development 4.a Build and upgrade education facilities that are child-, disability- and gender-sensitive and provide safe, non-violent, inclusive and effective learning environments for all 4.c By 2030, substantially increase the supply of qualified teachers, including through international co-operation for teacher training in developing countries

(Continued)

Table ES.1 The potential contribution of sport-based policy to the Global Sustainable Development Goal targets (*cont.*)

Goal	Target	
5 Gender equality	*Direct contribution*	5.1 End all forms of discrimination against all women and girls everywhere 5.5 Ensure women's full and effective participation and equal opportunities for leadership at all levels of decision making in political, economic and public life 5.c Adopt and strengthen sound policies and enforceable legislation for the promotion of gender equality and the empowerment of all women and girls at all levels
	Linked contribution	5.2 Eliminate all forms of violence against all women and girls in the public and private spheres, including trafficking and sexual and other types of exploitation 5.3 Eliminate all harmful practices, such as child, early and forced marriage and female genital mutilation
8 Decent work and economic growth	*Direct contribution*	8.6 By 2020, substantially reduce the proportion of youth not in employment, education or training
	Linked contribution	8.5 By 2030, achieve full and productive employment and decent work for all women and men, including for young people and persons with disabilities, and equal pay for work of equal value 8.3 Promote development-oriented policies that support productive activities, decent job creation, entrepreneurship, creativity and innovation, and encourage the formalisation and growth of micro-, small- and medium-sized enterprises, including through access to financial services 8.7 Take immediate and effective measures to eradicate forced labour, end modern slavery and human trafficking, and secure the prohibition and elimination of the worst forms of child labour, including recruitment and use of child soldiers, and by 2025 end child labour in all its forms 8.8 Protect labour rights and promote safe and secure working environments for all workers, including migrant workers, in particular women migrants, and those in precarious employment

(*Continued*)

Table ES.1 The potential contribution of sport-based policy to the Global Sustainable Development Goal targets (*cont.*)

Goal	Target	
11 Sustainable cities and communities	*Direct contribution*	11.7 By 2030, provide universal access to safe, inclusive and accessible, green and public spaces, in particular for women and children, older persons and persons with disabilities
	Linked contribution	11.3 By 2030, enhance inclusive and sustainable urbanisation and capacity for participatory, integrated and sustainable human settlement planning and management in all countries
16 Peace, justice and strong institutions	*Direct contribution*	16.2 End abuse, exploitation, trafficking and all forms of violence against and torture of children 16.6 Develop effective, accountable and transparent institutions at all levels 16.b Promote and enforce non-discriminatory laws and policies for sustainable development
	Linked contribution	16.1 Significantly reduce all forms of violence and related death rates everywhere 16.4 By 2030, significantly reduce illicit financial and arms flows, strengthen the recovery and return of stolen assets and combat all forms of organized crime 16.5 Substantially reduce corruption and bribery in all their forms 16.7 Ensure responsive, inclusive, participatory and representative decision making at all levels
17 Partnerships for the goals	*Means of implementation*	17.3 Mobilise additional financial resources for developing countries from multiple sources 17.14 Enhance policy coherence for sustainable development 17.15 Respect each country's policy space and leadership to establish and implement policies for poverty eradication and sustainable development multi-stakeholder partnerships

(*Continued*)

Table ES.1 The potential contribution of sport-based policy to the Global Sustainable Development Goal targets (*cont.*)

Goal	Target	
		17.16 Enhance the Global Partnership for Sustainable Development, complemented by multi-stakeholder partnerships that mobilize and share knowledge, expertise, technology and financial resources, to support the achievement of the Sustainable Development Goals in all countries, in particular developing countries 17.17 Encourage and promote effective public, public-private and civil society partnerships, building on the experience and resourcing strategies of partnerships
	Measuring progress	17.18 By 2020, enhance capacity-building support to developing countries, including for least developed countries and small island developing states, to increase significantly the availability of high-quality, timely and reliable data disaggregated by income, gender, age, race, ethnicity, migratory status, disability, geographical location and other characteristics relevant in national contexts 17.19 By 2030, build on existing initiatives to develop measurements of progress on sustainable development that complement gross domestic product, and support statistical capacity-building in developing countries

Source: UNGA (2015)

References

Dudfield, O. and M. Dingwall-Smith (2016), *Sport for Development and Peace and the 2030 Agenda for Sustainable Development Analysis Report*, Commonwealth Secretariat, London.

Kay, T. and O. Dudfield (2013), *The Commonwealth Guide to Advancing Development through Sport*, Commonwealth Secretariat, London, available at: http://assets.thecommonwealth.org/assetbank-commonwealth/action/viewAsset?id=23162andindex=3andtotal=11andview=viewSearchItem

UN General Assembly (UNGA) (2015), *Transforming our World: The 2030 Agenda for Sustainable Development*, available at: www.un.org/ga/search/view_doc.asp?symbol=A/70/L.1andLang=E

UNESCO (2013a), *Declaration of Berlin*, available at: http://unesdoc.unesco.org/images/0022/002211/221114e.pdf

UNESCO (2013b), *World-wide Survey of School Physical Education*, UNESCO, Paris, 19, available at: http://unesdoc.unesco.org/images/0022/002293/229335e.pdf

UNESCO (2015), *International Charter of Physical Education, Physical Activity and Sport*, available at: unesdoc.unesco.org/images/0023/002354/235409e.pdf

United Nations Conference on Housing and Sustainable Urban Development (2015), *Habitat III Issue Papers: 11 Public Space*, available at: http://unhabitat.org/wp-content/uploads/2015/04/Habitat-III-Issue-Paper-11_Public-Space-2.0.compressed.pdf

Contributors

Dr Iain Lindsey is Lecturer in Sport in the School of Applied Social Sciences, Durham University. Dr Lindsey has extensively researched Sport for Development in a number of different African contexts, and his interests also include analysis of youth sport policies and practices in the United Kingdom.

Professor Tony Chapman is Director of Policy & Practice at St Chad's College, Durham University. Professor Chapman's current interests focus on evaluation of the social impact of youth programmes and upon interactions between the public sector and voluntary sector.

Chapter 1 Sport and the Sustainable Development Goals

1.1 Introduction

The *2030 Agenda for Sustainable Development,* adopted by the United Nations General Assembly in September 2015, sets out a 'supremely ambitious and transformational vision' for global development (UNGA 2015). Central to the *2030 Agenda for Sustainable Development* are 17 SDGs broken down into 169 targets and 230 associated indicators (see Box 1.1). The SDGs seek to build on and complete progress towards the Millennium Development Goals (MDGs) that they replaced, but they are also more comprehensive and far-reaching in scope. The *2030 Agenda for Sustainable Development* emphasises that the SDGs are intended to be 'integrated and indivisible and balance the three dimensions of sustainable development: the economic, social and environmental' (UNGA 2015, preamble 1).

Central to the 2030 Agenda for Sustainable Development *are 17 SDGs broken down into 169 targets and 230 associated indicators.*

The *2030 Agenda for Sustainable Development* and SDGs also align with the *Charter of the Commonwealth,* which affirms the importance of sustainable development to 'eradicate poverty by pursuing inclusive growth whilst preserving and conserving natural ecosystems and promoting social equity' (Commonwealth Secretariat 2013). While the SDGs have been devised to be universally applicable, there is shared recognition in the *Commonwealth Charter* and the *2030 Agenda for Sustainable Development* of the particular needs of the least developed countries and small island states. There is further shared commitment to address the needs of the world's poorest and most vulnerable people, with young people among those prioritised. In this respect, both the *Charter* and *2030 Agenda for Sustainable Development* recognise the importance of creating opportunities and supportive environments through which young people can realise their own potential and actively contribute to sustainable development.

Box 1.1 Sustainable Development Goals

Goal 1. End poverty in all its forms everywhere

Goal 2. End hunger, achieve food security and improved nutrition and promote sustainable agriculture

Goal 3. Ensure healthy lives and promote well-being for all at all ages

Goal 4. Ensure inclusive and equitable quality education and promote lifelong learning opportunities for all

Goal 5. Achieve gender equality and empower all women and girls

Goal 6. Ensure availability and sustainable management of water and sanitation for all

Goal 7. Ensure access to affordable, reliable, sustainable and modern energy for all

Goal 8. Promote sustained, inclusive and sustainable economic growth, full and productive employment and decent work for all

Goal 9. Build resilient infrastructure, promote inclusive and sustainable industrialisation and foster innovation

Goal 10. Reduce inequality within and among countries

Goal 11. Make cities and human settlements inclusive, safe, resilient and sustainable

Goal 12. Ensure sustainable consumption and production patterns

Goal 13. Take urgent action to combat climate change and its impacts

Goal 14. Conserve and sustainably use the oceans, seas and marine resources for sustainable development

Goal 15. Protect, restore and promote sustainable use of terrestrial ecosystems, sustainably manage forests, combat desertification, halt and reverse land degradation and halt biodiversity loss

Goal 16. Promote peaceful and inclusive societies for sustainable development, provide access to justice for all and build effective, accountable and inclusive institutions at all levels

Goal 17. Strengthen the means of implementation and revitalise the Global Partnership for Sustainable Development

The potential for sport to contribute to sustainable development is explicitly stated in the 2030 Agenda for Sustainable Development.

The potential for sport to contribute to sustainable development is explicitly stated in the *2030 Agenda for Sustainable Development,* with identification of:

> *the growing contribution of sport to the realization of development and peace in its promotion of tolerance and respect and the contributions it makes to the empowerment of women and of young people, individuals and communities as well as to health, education and social inclusion objectives.*
>
> (UNGA 2015, para. 37, 10)

This statement extends previous key international declarations that recognise and advocate the use of sport as a catalyst

Figure 1.1 International declarations, policies and publications on Sport for Development and Peace

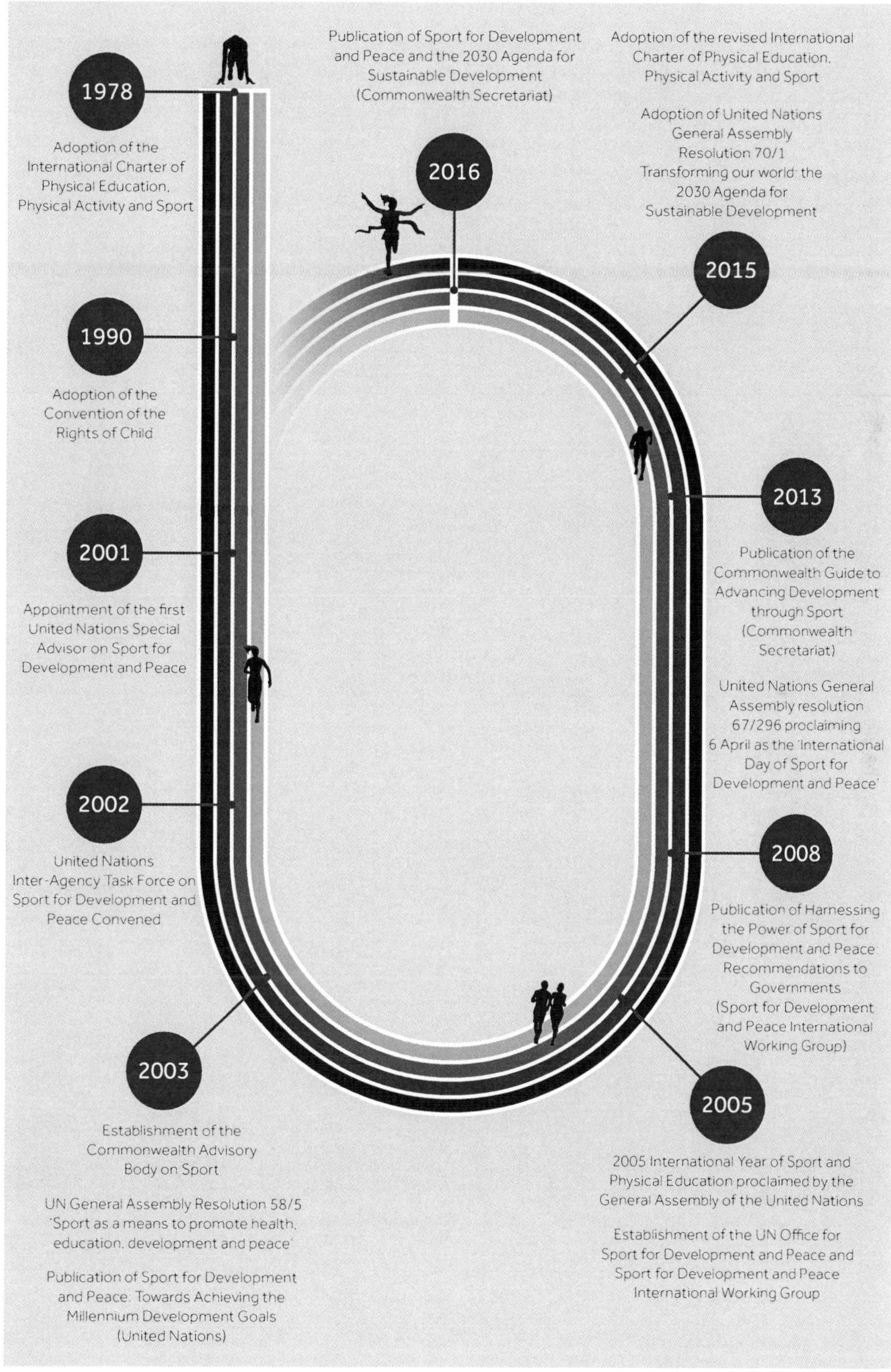

for human and social development (see Figure 1.1). Nine such resolutions were passed by the United Nations General Assembly between 2003 and 2014 (See list of website resources). In this same period, Commonwealth governments also provided consistent endorsement of the role of sport in contributing to development and peace across multiple Commonwealth Sports Ministers Meetings and at the 2011 Commonwealth Heads of Government Meeting (Commonwealth Secretariat 2011).

This guide provides direction for governmental policy-makers and other stakeholders to enable sport to make the fullest possible contribution to sustainable development.

The period since the introduction of the MDGs, therefore, has been one in which there has been increasing recognition of the contribution of sport to development agendas. The *2030 Agenda for Sustainable Development* represents a further important milestone for sport but also brings significant responsibility for all stakeholders to collectively contribute to global aspirations. This guide provides direction for governmental policy-makers and other stakeholders to enable sport to make the fullest possible contribution to sustainable development. Beginning with the following section, and throughout the following chapters, the guide is based on sound, balanced and evidenced analysis, both of existing practice in sport and of policy options that can enable further progress towards sustainable development.

1.2 Sport and sustainable development: Existing contributions to policy and practice

Since the millennium, a significant number and range of policy and practice interventions have sought to enhance the contribution of sport to sustainable development. The international policy impetus provided by the United Nations, Commonwealth and other multilateral institutions has been complemented in individual countries by interventions at different levels of government that have facilitated and framed the implementation of sport-based approaches to development. Global commitments and governmental policies, where present, have been accompanied by widespread expansion in the contribution of a variety of civil society organisations, sport federations and private sector organisations to the resourcing and delivery of numerous sport-based initiatives. Continued policy development, therefore, requires a detailed understanding of the existing landscape of sport-based approaches to development and appreciation of the ongoing fluidity that characterises a rapidly developing sector.

1.2.1 The Commonwealth and the United Nations system

Leadership provided through the Commonwealth and the United Nations system, and by other multi-national institutions, has been instrumental in guiding the global emergence and establishment of Sport for Development and Peace. The appointment of the UN's first Special Advisor on Sport for Development and Peace in 2001, and the establishment of the UN Office for Sport for Development and Peace in 2005, enabled sport to become better established within and across the UN system. From *Sport for Development and Peace: Towards Achieving the Millennium Development Goals* in 2003 to *Harnessing the Power of Sport for Development and Peace: Recommendations to Governments* in 2008, various policy documents published through the UN system and its associated bodies (see list of website resources) have played an important role in establishing global frameworks for sport and development.

Leadership provided through the Commonwealth and the United Nations system, and by other multi-national institutions, has been instrumental in guiding the global emergence and establishment of Sport for Development and Peace.

There has been interest across the UN system in the value of sport as a tool that could be used innovatively and symbiotically with interventions in other sectors to address a range of development agendas. During the period preceding the *2030 Agenda for Sustainable Development*, specific policy documents highlighted the potential contribution of sport across all eight of the MDGs (UNOSDP 2010). UNESCO (United Nations Education, Scientific and Cultural Organization) member states adopted both the *Declaration of Berlin* in 2013 and a revised *International Charter of Physical Education, Physical Activity and Sport* in 2015 that further emphasise the importance of inclusive opportunities for all to participate in sport, and of efforts to combat threats to the integrity of sport. Besides global commitments and evidence-based documentation, sharing of effective policies and practice for sport-based approaches has also been furthered by UN bodies and other multilateral institutions through the organisation of global conferences and dissemination of documented examples.

1.2.2 National governments

Selected national governments have increasingly endorsed and provided various forms of support for sport-based approaches to development, with Commonwealth countries often being at the forefront of such initiatives.

Over time, selected national governments have increasingly endorsed and provided various forms of support for sport-based approaches to development, with Commonwealth countries often being at the forefront of such initiatives (Giulianotti

2014). There is diversity across countries with regard to the location of sport within national governmental structures. A minority of countries have specific ministries for sport. More commonly, governments' policy role for sport has been shaped by its positioning within broader ministries, such as those for young people, education, health or culture. Within these ministries, responsibility for sport in relation to development has typically been assigned to departments and national public bodies whose existing remits also include grass-roots and elite sport development. Partly as a consequence of these differing governmental structures, processes of national policy development can differ in respect of the extent of integration between sport and broader governmental priorities, such as those for education and health (Keim and de Coning 2014).

Sub-national and local governments can and do also make significant contributions to sport and development. However, the substantial diversity in sub-national and local governmental structures across and within countries means that any overarching analysis or policy prescriptions need to be offered with caution. The extent of decentralisation and also the level of coherence between national, sub-national and local priorities for sport need to be considered on a country-specific basis. Nevertheless, sub-national and local governments may have significant roles in infrastructure planning that can have significant implications for sport (Nicholson *et al.* 2010). At these levels of government, further attention can also be given to ensuring that the implementation of sport-based initiatives is appropriately resourced and effectively targeted towards specific community needs.

1.2.3 Civil society organisations

Civil society organisations have been particularly prominent in the emergence of sport-based approaches to development.

Civil society organisations have been particularly prominent in the emergence of sport-based approaches to development and, in increasing numbers, make a substantial contribution to the implementation of particular initiatives. A vital consideration for policy-makers is the range and diversity of civil society organisations that now exist across and within particular countries. Some major and now well-established international non-governmental organisations (NGOs) have, over time, contributed to sport and development across multiple countries through building networks, developing specific sport-based curricula and providing funding and other resources (Giulianotti 2014).

Similar forms of support are also provided by more recently emergent international NGOs that initially tend to be more reliant on the work of volunteers and so operate across a more limited range of countries (Svensson and Hambrick 2016). In-country NGOs vary similarly in scale, scope and operation (Giulianotti 2011). Many have emerged locally through the commitment and contribution of local activists, and some early in-country NGOs have expanded, sometimes with international support, to deliver sport-based activities across a variety of localities. Others remain small-scale, operating within specific communities and without or with only limited international support (Lindsey 2016).

The diversity of international and in-country NGOs is matched by significant variation in their established and emerging approaches to sport and development provision. Collectively, these approaches encompass different forms of sport, play, traditional games and other physical activities. Some organisations and approaches are specifically oriented towards specific issues (e.g. HIV/AIDS), while others use more holistic and flexible approaches to contribute to efforts to address a range of development outcomes. As a result, scope for increased alignment between NGOs and other sport and development stakeholders varies according to the extent to which the identification of common goals may be feasible (Sanders *et al.* 2014). A further relevant aspect of the work of NGOs is their common focus on targeted communities and with groups of young people who may be considered particularly vulnerable (Coalter and Taylor 2010). The feasibility and also desirability of scaling-up NGO provision is therefore an appropriate consideration for policy-makers.

The diversity of international and in-country NGOs is matched by significant variation in their established and emerging approaches to sport and development provision.

1.2.4 Sport federations

A variety of international, national and local sport federations and bodies have also increasingly contributed to efforts to use sport as a tool for sustainable development. Both the International Olympic Committee (IOC) and the Commonwealth Games Federation (CGF) have strongly engaged with sport-based approaches to development; as a result, their understanding of and commitment to the utilisation of sport events to lever sustainable social, economic and environmental legacies has been strengthened. International sport-specific federations have also contributed to sport-based approaches in similar ways through their own events, by sponsoring specific initiatives and via the use of high-profile athletes who serve as advocates, ambassadors and role models (Akindes and Kirwan 2009).

There can be challenges in aligning competitive and selective notions of sport development and performance with more inclusive approaches that use sport to address development objectives.

Many national sport federations and their local member clubs have also either delivered their own sport-based initiatives or worked in partnership with NGOs to do so (Giulianotti 2011a). Sport federations and bodies at all levels also have valuable expertise in the development of sport that can be applied to development objectives. In some instances, however, there can be challenges in aligning competitive and selective notions of sport development and performance with more inclusive approaches that use sport to address development objectives (Akindes and Kirwan 2009). Furthermore, efforts to contribute to development outcomes may be weakened if sports federations and their events become associated with high-profile doping, corruption or governance scandals.

1.2.5 Private-sector organisations

Increasing recognition of the contributions that private sector organisations can make to sport-based approaches to development has come as their global prominence has grown.

Increasing recognition of the contributions that private sector organisations can make to sport-based approaches to development has come as their global prominence has grown. However, private-sector support is by no means uniform; as yet this has tended to coalesce around particular clusters of activity and types of organisation. Major transnational companies associated with sport and other industries have both undertaken their own sport and development campaigns and provided funding for delivery of initiatives by NGOs (Levermore 2010). Smaller-scale sponsorship by private-sector organisations has long provided important resources for the development of community sport in some contexts, although the potential to generate income from similar sources has yet to be substantially realised in relation to sport and development specifically.

The wider roles and contributions of the private sector within the overall sport industry also require consideration. Securing the economic impact and legacies of both large- and smaller-scale sporting events requires leverage of the benefits of private-sector involvement. More generally, private-sector employment across the sport industry can also contribute to economic development. National governments have, on occasions, however, been called on to address concerns with the employment practices of transnational sport businesses (Thibault 2009). In contrast, locally focused models of social enterprise in sport have more recently emerged and begun to spread across different countries and contexts. Finally, private media organisations are hugely influential in promoting and shaping perceptions of sport. There remains significant and underexplored potential for the capacities of mass-communication media to be harnessed to enhance the contribution of sport to sustainable development (Keim and de Coning 2014).

There remains significant and underexplored potential for the capacities of mass-communication media to be harnessed to enhance the contribution of sport to sustainable development.

1.3 Commonwealth policy guidance for sport and sustainable development

Commonwealth sports ministers, the Commonwealth Secretariat and the Commonwealth Advisory Body on Sports have made ongoing commitments to support governments and other key stakeholders to collectively utilise sport in the service of development and building peaceful and inclusive communities. Resulting from these commitments, the *Commonwealth Guide to Advancing Development through Sport* provided a 'nuanced, measured and credible account' that drew on evidence and learning from across sport and development (Kay and Dudfield 2013). It established six key principles upon which policies and practices for sport-based approaches to development can be based (see Box 1.2).

The Commonwealth Guide to Advancing Development through Sport *provided a 'nuanced, measured and credible account' that drew on evidence and learning from across sport and development.*

Box 1.2 Six principles for advancing development through sport

Principle 1: Sport for Development and Peace must be explicitly linked to the Commonwealth's shared values and commitment to promoting development, democracy and diversity.

Principle 2: Sport for Development and Peace should leverage sustainable, quality and ongoing sport activity and be intentionally planned to realise specific developmental goals.

Principle 3: Sport for Development and Peace is most effective when integrated with the development sector in support of regional, national and local development priorities.

Principle 4: Fully accessible programmes ensuring leaders and participants are safeguarded at all times.

Principle 5: Decentralised programmes that involve intended beneficiaries and their communities in the planning process and take local needs and assets into consideration.

Principle 6: Programmes designed on the basis of evidence-based models, and conducted with systematic measurement of progress and appropriate monitoring and evaluation.

The emphasis that these six principles give to various aspects of policy design, implementation and evaluation is strongly aligned with the priority given within the *2030 Agenda for Sustainable Development* to strengthening the means of implementation required to achieve all SDGs. This is especially encapsulated in SDG 17, which emphasises policy coherence, country-leadership, multi-sectoral partnerships, mobilisation of financial and human resources, and measurement of progress towards all SDGs. The importance accorded to SDG 17, and its alignment with existing Commonwealth principles, therefore, centrally underpins this guide. Section One draws on analysis of SDG 17 targets to present frameworks for policy implementation and for reviewing and monitoring where sport may make contributions to sustainable development.

Section Two utilises these frameworks to inform identification of policy options that can serve to enhance the contribution of sport across specific SDGs associated with health (SDG 3); education (SDG 4); gender (SDG 5); economic growth and employment (SDG 8); cities and human settlements (SDG 11); and peaceful and just societies and institutions (SDG 16). These have been identified through extensive consultation, led by the Commonwealth Secretariat, as those goals to which sport-based approaches can make effective and cost-efficient contributions. Throughout Section Two, this guide therefore builds on the Commonwealth Analysis of *Sport for Development and Peace and the 2030 Agenda for Sustainable Development* (Commonwealth Secretariat 2016) to support further evidence-based policy development towards each of these six SDGs.

References

Akindes, G. and M. Kirwan (2009), 'Sport as international aid: assisting development or promoting under-development in Sub-Saharan Africa?', in Levermore, R. and A. Beacom (Eds), *Sport and International Development*, Macmillan, Basingtoke, 215–245.

Coalter, F. and J. Taylor (2010), *Sport-for-Development Impact Study. A Research Initiative funded by Comic Relief and UK Sport and managed by International Development through Sport*, available at: http://www.uksport.gov.uk/docLib/MISC/FredCoalterseminalMandEManual.pdf

Commonwealth Secretariat (2011), *Commonwealth Heads of Government Meeting Communiqué*, Perth, Australia, available at: http://thecommonwealth.org/media/news/commonwealth-leaders-release-chogm-2011-communiqu%C3%A9#sthash.07kJPEq2.dpuf

Commonwealth Secretariat (2013), Charter of the *Commonwealth*, available at: www.thecommonwealth.org/our-charter

Commonwealth Secretariat (2016), *Sport for Development and Peace and the 2030 Agenda for Sustainable Development Analysis Report*, Commonwealth Secretariat, London.

Giulianotti, R. (2011), The sport, development and peace sector: a model of four social policy domains', *Journal of Social Policy*, Vol. 40 issue 4, 757–76.

Giulianotti, R. (2014), 'Sport for Development and Peace Policy Options in the Commonwealth', in Dudfield, O. (Ed.), *Strengthening Sport for Development and Peace. National Policies and Strategies*, Commonwealth Secretariat, London.

Kay, T. and O. Dudfield (2013), *The Commonwealth Guide to Advancing Development through Sport*, Commonwealth Secretariat, London, available at: http://assets.thecommonwealth.org/assetbank-commonwealth/action/viewAsset?id=23162andindex=3andtotal=11andview=viewSearchItem

Keim, M. and C. de Coning (Eds) (2014), *Sport and Development Policy in Africa: Results of a Collaborative Study of Selected Country Cases*, SUN Press, Stellenbosch.

Levermore, R. (2010), 'CSR for development through sport: Examining its potential and limitations', *Third World Quarterly*, Vol. 31, 223–241.

Lindsey, I. (2016), 'Governance in Sport-for-Development: Problems and possibilities of (not) learning from international development', *International Review for the Sociology of Sport*, available at: http://irs.sagepub.com/content/early/2016/01/05/1012690215623460.abstract

Nicholson, M., R. Hoye and B. Houlihan (Eds) (2010), *Participation in Sport: International Policy Perspectives*, Routledge, Abingdon.

Sanders, B., J. Phillips and B. Vanreusel (2014), 'Opportunities and challenges facing NGOs using sport as a vehicle for development in post-apartheid South Africa', *Sport, Education and Society*, Vol. 19, 789–805.

Svensson, P. G. and M. E. Hambrick (2016), '"Pick and choose our battles": Understanding organizational capacity in a sport for development and peace organization', *Sport Management Review*, Vol. 19, 120–132.

Thibault, L. (2009), 'Globalization of sport: an inconvenient truth', *Journal of Sport Management*, Vol. 23, 1–20.

United Nations General Assembly (UNGA) (2015), *Transforming our World: The 2030 Agenda for Sustainable Development*, available at: www.un.org/ga/search/view_doc.asp?symbol=A/70/L.1andLang=E

UNESCO (2013), *Declaration of Berlin*, available at: http://unesdoc.unesco.org/images/0022/002211/221114e.pdf

UNESCO (2015) *International Charter of Physical Education, Physical Activity and Sport*, available at: unesdoc.unesco.org/images/0023/002354/235409e.pdf

United Nations Office on Sport for Development and Peace (UNOSDP) (2010), *Contribution of Sport to the Millennium Development Goals*, available at: http://www.un.org/wcm/webdav/site/sport/shared/sport/pdfs/Backgrounders/Sport%20and%20the%20MDGs_FACTSHEET_February%202010.pdf

Website Resources

International Platform on Sport and Development: www.sportanddev.org

http://www.un.org/wcm/content/site/sport/home/resourcecenter/publications

http://www.un.org/wcm/content/site/sport/home/resourcecenter/resolutions/pid/19431

Section One

Sustainable Development Goal 17: Strengthen the Means of Implementation and Revitalise the Global Partnership for Sustainable Development

Chapter 2
Introduction to Sustainable Development Goal 17

Realising the scale and ambition of the *2030 Agenda for Sustainable Development* requires commitment to providing the means of implementation by which the SDGs can be achieved. This is reflected in the importance accorded to SDG 17 and its associated targets. Intensive global engagement across the United Nations system, bringing together governments, civil society and private sector actors, is promised so as to mobilise all available resources for sustainable development.

Intensive global engagement across the United Nations system, bringing together governments, civil society and private sector actors, is promised so as to mobilise all available resources for sustainable development.

While seeking to enhance the Global Partnership for Sustainable Development, the 2030 Agenda for Sustainable Development strongly and consistently reiterates that:

> *each country has primary responsibility for its own economic and social development and that the role of national policies and development strategies cannot be overemphasized.*
>
> (UNGA 2015)

The means of implementation, therefore, need to be considered and strengthened within each country, alongside the global impetus to be provided by the United Nations system, through the auspices of the Commonwealth, and by other multilateral actors. As stated in Chapter 1, this guide also focuses on policies that can be implemented by country governments to enhance the contribution of sport to sustainable development. Aspects of SDG 17 are recognised as key to this contribution and underpin policy options identified in respect of specific SDGs in Section Two of this guide.

Informing these policy options is the analysis, presented in Chapter 3, of the relevance to governments and sport stakeholders of the SDG 17 targets associated with country-leadership and policy coherence, mobilising financial and human resources, and multi-stakeholder and cross-sectoral partnerships. This analysis leads to the presentation of a framework of approaches to implementation that can enhance the collective contribution of sport to sustainable development, and specific goals and targets.

SDG 17 targets for data, monitoring and accountability are associated with the primary responsibility that governments have for reviewing progress towards implementing and achieving the SDGs. Effective policy-making is reliant on access to reliable, high-quality and disaggregated data. Chapter 4 analyses current approaches to monitoring, evaluating and evidencing sport-based approaches. From this analysis, Chapter 4 identifies potential methods and important considerations for policy-makers who have responsibility for reviewing the contribution of sport to the SDGs.

Reference

UN General Assembly (UNGA) (2015), *Transforming our World: The 2030 Agenda for Sustainable Development*, available at: www.un.org/ga/search/view_doc.asp?symbol=A/70/L.1andLang=E

Chapter 3
Means of Implementation (SDG 17)

3.1 Introduction

An array of public, private and civil society organisations have sought to utilise sport to contribute to sustainable development. The *2030 Agenda for Sustainable Development*, and SDG17, similarly and more broadly recognise the need for collective approaches that bring together governments, the private sector and civil society in implementing the SDGs. Consequently, this guide gives strong priority to collective approaches to enhance the contribution of sport across the range of SDGs and to address a number of SDG 17 targets.

The 2030 Agenda for Sustainable Development, and SDG17, similarly and more broadly recognise the need for collective approaches that bring together governments, the private sector and civil society in implementing the SDGs.

Together, SDG targets 17.14 and 17.15 establish the significance of country-leadership for policy coherence across different development agendas and organisations. The associated importance of effective mobilisation of resources held by different organisations and co-operation in building human resource capacity, is emphasised through SDG targets 17.3 and 17.9, respectively. The importance of multi-stakeholder partnerships to sport-based approaches has previously been recognised in policy and practice, but further progress remains a priority with respect to specific SDG targets 17.16 and 17.17.

Policy implementation can draw upon different configurations and partnerships of public, private and civil society organisations. Oriented by preceding analysis of those SDG 17 targets identified above, this chapter identifies a framework of approaches to enhance the collective contribution of sport to sustainable development. This framework encompasses implementation approaches that are government led; are structured through formal partnerships between public and private or civil society organisations; enhance mutual support through complementary actions; and draw on the autonomous contributions of different organisations.

This chapter identifies a framework of approaches to enhance the collective contribution of sport to sustainable development.

The analysis and framework presented in this chapter underpins specific policy options that are identified subsequently in this guide in respect of specific SDGs.

Recognition of the possibilities and implications of this framework enables policy-makers to consider context-specific approaches to using sport to contribute to sustainable development. As such, the analysis and framework presented in this chapter underpins specific policy options that are identified subsequently in this guide in respect of specific SDGs.

3.2 Analysis of sport and specific SDG targets

Target 17.14 Enhance policy coherence for sustainable development.

Target 17.15 Respect each country's policy space and leadership to establish and implement policies for poverty eradication and sustainable development.

Country-leadership offers the potential to enhance policy coherence, in order to strengthen the contribution of sport to sustainable development.

Country-leadership offers the potential to enhance policy coherence, in order to strengthen the contribution of sport to sustainable development. Diverse public, private and civil society organisations may support, fund and deliver sport-based approaches that seek to contribute towards sustainable development. Articulation of national policy priorities can enable these various sport and development organisations to work collectively towards identified and shared goals (SDPIWG 2008; Lindsey 2016). Furthermore, the qualities of flexibility and innovation that can serve to enhance the contribution of sport can be most effectively harnessed through country-leadership that recognises the specific socio-cultural context of sport and its relationship to national development priorities. Appropriately decentralised policy leadership can ensure that planning for sport and development takes full account of local conditions and the particular needs and assets of intended beneficiaries (Kay and Dudfield 2013).

The potential contribution of sport is also best realised through multi-level alignment and integration with policy developments in other sectors, such as education, health and economic development. Achieving this level of policy coherence may be challenging in some contexts (Keim and de Coning 2014) and requires a substantial measure of mutual understanding and adaptation across the range of policy actors. Greater flexibility for the recognition and incorporation of sport-based approaches may especially be required where national policy frameworks in other sectors are already well established (Lindsey and Banda 2011). Equally, sport policy stakeholders may assess the national and local development objectives to which sport-based approaches can most effectively contribute, in order to prioritise integration with identified sectors, rather than dilute and diversify impact (Coalter 2010).

Enhancing policy coherence also requires recognition of complexities associated with different priorities within the sport sector. There is great potential in achieving within-sector synergies between grass-roots, elite sport and Sport for Development and Peace, but policy impetus may be required to balance and, where possible, reconcile interests associated with different areas of sport (Nicholson *et al.* 2010). Systematic and highly focused strategies for the development of competitive, high-performance sport do not automatically align with decentralised approaches that can best realise benefits derived through participation in sport and other forms of physical activity (Hayhurst and Frisby 2010). Greater synergies may be encouraged through demonstrating how addressing issues of relevance to sport and development, such as inequalities in participation, may also bring benefits to sport federations and other established sport stakeholders.

Enhancing policy coherence also requires recognition of complexities associated with different priorities within the sport sector.

The increasing influence of globalisation across many aspects of sport also presents opportunities and challenges for efforts to enhance national policy coherence. The potential for policy learning and transfer across countries has been well-realised in respect of high-performance sport, and many transnational opportunities for sharing sport and development practice have also been created (see, for example, the International Platform on Sport and Development, www.sportanddev.org). Funding available from international organisations has also significantly contributed to aspects of sport and development provision, especially in countries with significant resource constraints. International funding can be best utilised within the frames provided by country-led policies to address concerns that sport-based approaches have been undermined by funders' top-down implementation of standardised approaches to practice and accountability (Kay 2012; Darnell 2014).

Promoting the role of sport in national development in Zambia

Zambia

Bessie Malilwe Chelemu
Director of Sport
Ministry of Youth, Sport and Child Development
Government of Zambia

Young people below the age of 35 make up 82 per cent of the Zambian population. This kind of population distribution presents challenges for promoting social and economic development, particularly for meeting the needs of young people. Sport can play a role in addressing these issues if supported by the implementation of appropriate development-orientated sport policy.

Zambia's second National Sports Policy, developed in 2006 and amended in 2012, took into consideration emerging issues such as gender, anti-doping and the commercialisation of sport. Recognising that sport can make a broader contribution to national and international sustainable development priorities, and in order to identify how best to maximise this potential, the Ministry of Youth, Sport and Child Development undertook a review of the national sport policy in 2016.

In working to align sport policy direction with the country's development priorities, the following emerging policy objectives, not included in the 2012 National Sports Policy, were identified and are important to help create an enabling environment to ensure that sport can make a meaningful contribution to national development.

- Enhancing the role of sport in improving physical and mental health and well-being and promoting social cohesion and social integration at both the community and national levels.
- Recognising the role of sport in creating opportunities for young people, improving employability and generating income and thus mobilising human, financial and physical resources to increase the viability, sustainability and growth of the sport sector to enhance its contribution to gross national product.
- Encouraging educational institutions to develop and implement innovative and appropriate courses of study that support the sport industry, and creating awareness through public education campaigns. Of particular note is the certification of non-traditional and emerging careers in sport to provide more formal recognition of the transferable skills young people develop volunteering or working in Zambia's well-developed sport NGO sector.
- Strengthening the governance of sport in the country to create an environment in which both sports organisations and the broader community can effectively engage with sport as a tool for social and economic development.

In identifying these priorities, the Zambia Government's intention was to provide clearer strategic focus and policy direction for all stakeholders on the development priorities that sport can contribute to in the country. A specific goal was to strengthen alignment with national development priorities, in particular Zambia's Vision 2030 and the Seventh National Development Plan, which was developed in 2016.

(Continued)

Promoting the role of sport in national development in Zambia (*cont.*)

A number of the key objectives of this national development plan impacted on the sport policy revision process, notably the need to enhance the role of sports in promoting economic diversification and job creation, enhancing Zambia's human capital and creating a conducive governance environment in the country. A focus on reducing development inequality, and an emphasis on mainstreaming gender issues and protecting the rights of children and people with a disability were particularly important reference points. Efforts to align the revised sports policy to the National Development Plan aligns with SDG target 17.4, which highlights the need to enhance policy coherence for sustainable development.

A key challenge will be for the Zambia Government to work in partnership with sporting organisations, the private sector and civil society to ensure the envisaged policy direction can be implemented and policy coherence and programme co-ordination is achieved. To do this, further resource mobilisation, partnerships and the robust monitoring and evaluation of results achieved will be priorities for the Zambia Government moving forward.

Target 17.3 Mobilise additional financial resources for developing countries from multiple sources.

Target 17.9 Enhance international support for implementing effective and targeted capacity-building in developing countries to support national plans to implement all the Sustainable Development Goals, including through North–South, South–South and triangular co-operation.

Effective and enhanced marshalling of financial and human resources is vital to maximising the contribution of sport to the SDGs. The emergence of many sport-based initiatives has been driven by a committed, diverse and geographically spread base of activists, often working within stringent funding constraints (Kidd 2008; Giulianotti 2011a). In many countries, resources are insufficient to fully scale sport-based approaches, and government funding is often stretched over multiple priorities within and beyond sport. Among these priorities, elite sport may often be most adequately resourced at the national level (Dudfield 2014; Nicholson *et al.* 2010). Further analyses of the distribution of sport funding can often indicate additional inequities associated with gender, class, disability and geography.

The emergence of many sport-based initiatives has been driven by a committed, diverse and geographically spread base of activists, often working within stringent funding constraints.

For international and in-country NGOs that are often at the forefront of the implementation of sport-based initiatives, funding is a particularly prominent and ongoing issue. There are significant variations in the resource base across the

Well-established policy frameworks can be helpful to SDG NGOs in working towards developing a more sustainable funding base.

diversity of sport and development NGOs (Giulianotti 2011a; Lindsey 2016). Some have successfully and innovatively diversified their funding sources and, in so doing, have managed to cement and expand their sport and development operations. Others operate under more precarious funding conditions, and in-country NGOs, especially, have faced challenges in attempting to diversify and strengthen their resource base when broader economic conditions are restrictive (Giulianotti 2014; Lindsey 2016). Well-established policy frameworks can be helpful to such NGOs in working towards developing a more sustainable funding base which, in turn, can alleviate recognised problems associated with dependency and mission drift (Coalter 2010; Darnell 2014).

Especially given the issues with respect to the scale and nature of financial resources, priority must continue to be given to recruiting individuals to lead and deliver sport-based approaches, and to developing the skills that they require to do so. Capacity-building has been especially prominent in many North–South sport and development initiatives, although there are fewer examples of similarly focused South–South partnerships as yet (Darnell and Huish 2015). Across sport and development, various documented resources and models now exist to guide training programmes (Cronin 2011), and a number of initiatives have built capacity among cohorts of in-country trainers who can then cascade training locally to those who may be involved in leading the delivery of specific sport-based activities. The planning and design of all such capacity-building initiatives is significantly enhanced when undertaken collaboratively with local practitioners who have significant expertise and knowledge of sport and development delivery (Wright *et al.* 2016).

Addressing constraints that limit the scale and sustainability of capacity-building may also enhance the long-term contribution of sport to sustainable development. Many capacity-building initiatives are narrowly, if pragmatically, targeted and focused towards volunteers and young people. The suitability of sport as a potential environment for youth development and leadership has been particularly well realised (Schulenkorf *et al.* 2016). Placing significant responsibility on young volunteers to sustain sport-based provision can present difficulties. Especially in resource-constrained environments, expectations for young people to contribute materially to their families can inhibit long-term volunteering (Hasselgård and Straume 2015). In isolation, few sport-based initiatives have, as yet, been effective in establishing varied and comprehensive progression routes that are suitable for a range of young leaders to follow across different transitions in their lives.

Target 17.16 Enhance the Global Partnership for Sustainable Development, complemented by multi-stakeholder partnerships that mobilise and share knowledge, expertise, technology and financial resources, to support the achievement of the Sustainable Development Goals in all countries, in particular developing countries.

Target 17.17 Encourage and promote effective public, public-private and civil society partnerships, building on the experience and resourcing strategies of partnerships.

At all levels of policy and practice, there is consistent recognition of, but also further scope to realise, the significant potential of cross-sectoral partnerships that can support the contribution of sport to development outcomes. This is vital given that the wide variety of sport stakeholders is often matched by similar diversity across associated development sectors. Existing sport and development partnerships have taken multiple forms and have been oriented by different purposes (Lindsey and Banda 2011; Sanders *et al.* 2014). However, duplication and unnecessary competition has hindered the collective effectiveness of sport and development in a number of contexts (Giulianotti 2011b; Kidd 2011). Limitations of partnerships across international, national and local stakeholders can contribute to inefficiencies in the use of resources and can hinder the implementation of contextually relevant sport-based provision (Black 2010).

At all levels of policy and practice, there is consistent recognition of, but also further scope to realise, the significant potential of cross-sectoral partnerships that can support the contribution of sport to development outcomes.

Numerous, discrete examples of sport and development partnerships are readily identifiable, many of which are instigated to support specific sport-based initiatives. International and in-country NGOs have commonly worked in partnership to enhance resources for locally led sport-based provision. Sport federations at different levels have joined with other sport and development organisations to contribute to particular initiatives. Partnerships between sport-oriented organisations and those from other development sectors have also enhanced the delivery of initiatives through the utilisation of different skills, knowledge and expertise (Lindsey and Banda 2011). There is not, however, uniform involvement of all sport and development organisations across the range of identified partnerships. Some newer and smaller NGOs may not be well linked into networks through which partnerships can be developed, and such NGOs may also lack the capacity required for partnership instigation and development (Lindsey 2016). Furthermore, the time-limited nature of some sport-based initiatives can lead to difficulty in sustaining associated partnerships in the longer term.

There can be particular benefits but also specific challenges in developing and engaging in partnerships with a wider scale, membership or scope than those associated with specific sport-based initiatives. In a number of Commonwealth countries, commitments have been made to instigate partnerships across a broad representation of governmental and non-governmental stakeholders involved in sport and development (see, for example, Department Sport and Recreation South Africa 2011; Lindsey 2016, in respect of Ghana and Tanzania). Such multi-stakeholder partnerships can involve significant complexities as a result of the different capacities of the stakeholders involved, and the need to balance co-operation with organisational independence. As a result, moving from dialogue within sport and development networks to develop deeper integration and synergies has, in some instances, proved a challenging aspiration (Lindsey 2016). Likewise, structural constraints that can, for example, create competition for funding may need to be addressed to enable greater integration of sport agencies into multi-stakeholder partnerships instigated to enhance co-ordination within other development sectors.

3.3 Enhancing collective impact: A framework for sport and development policy options

A diverse array of public, private and civil society organisations – both within and outside the sport sector, and working at levels from the international to local – can make important contributions towards the SDGs.

The advent of the *2030 Agenda for Sustainable Development* and the importance accorded to the associated means of implementation provide an important opportunity for policy development that is aligned with the possibilities – and also the challenges – identified in the preceding analysis. Again, a diverse array of public, private and civil society organisations – both within and outside the sport sector, and working at levels from the international to local – can make important contributions towards the SDGs. Disparate individual interventions by any agency can enable positive change, and yet greater potential resides in enabling collective contributions towards commonly recognised and prioritised goals. Approaches across different agencies can mobilise resources in ways that are collectively effective and efficient. Collective approaches to implementation can be more sustainable than isolated initiatives. Developing policy coherence at levels from the national to local can both enhance and be enhanced by collective approaches within the sport sector and across the development sectors associated with particular SDGs.

Collective approaches to implementation can be more sustainable than isolated initiatives.

The principle of collective endeavour towards shared goals is therefore appealing, but it would be naive to expect a wide range of agencies from different sectors to marshal their resources of money, people and ideas in an entirely unified way. Likewise, it may be detrimental if public institutions attempt to structure, manage or procedurally constrain autonomous agencies that independently foster positive change. Policy responses to these complexities need to be carefully considered if they are to encourage collective contributions towards common objectives. To support policy-makers in this task, Table 3.1 identifies a framework of four approaches to collective implementation, with associated sport and development examples, that may be enacted to harness sport in the service of making the fullest possible contribution to the SDGs.

It may be detrimental if public institutions attempt to structure, manage or procedurally constrain autonomous agencies that independently foster positive change.

Table 3.1 Framework of approaches to collective implementation

Approach	Description	Examples
Government-led implementation	Independent government-led implementation may include direct provision of services and independent regulation of non-governmental actors operating within the government's legitimate spheres of influence. Such interventions can have the potential to operate at scale, ensure equity across different populations or mitigate harmful practices. Achievement of stated objectives depends largely upon the capacity and capability of national, regional or local public-sector institutions that are responsible for government-led implementation. Conversely, there are risks of harm to existing non-governmental provision if ambitions for government-led implementation outstrip the means available to enact them	• Provision of physical education across all state schools • Enforcement of anti-corruption, child protection or labour laws within sport

(Continued)

Table 3.1 Framework of approaches to collective implementation (*cont.*)

Approach	Description	Examples
Structured implementation partnerships	Structured partnerships are formal relationships, usually with support and/or funding from government, within which configurations of public, private or civil society agencies can collectively contribute to improved policy co-ordination and the delivery of services to achieve specific agreed objectives. The success of such partnerships remains dependent upon government's capacity to generate sufficient resource and/or frame approaches to practice that can produce the stated objectives. Unless provision is universal and alternative provision is prohibited through legislation, there is a likelihood that non-government agencies may also deliver initiatives that continue alongside structured implementation partnerships	• Public funding for national sport federations and other sport-based organisations to deliver specific agreed objectives • Development of common quality standards for aspects of sport-based provision
Complementary implementation	Complementary implementation can involve agencies from the public, private and civil society sectors where common goals can be, in some meaningful way, collectively achieved, and where initiatives are co-produced or delivered semi-autonomously to achieve commonly recognised outcomes. Complementary implementation can draw on agencies' different mandates and varied human and financial resources in mutually supportive ways. Arrangements for complementary implementation are necessarily entered into voluntarily and require reciprocal relationships which are underpinned by dialogue and measures of mutual trust and confidence	• Specific initiatives to build capacity across public, private and voluntary sector agencies • Contributions of sport-based organisations to implementation of specific initiatives within other development sectors, such as public health or education
Autonomous implementation	Autonomous implementation operates through self-determined initiatives developed by private or civil society agencies. Ideally, such initiatives align with policy objectives instituted or recognised by governmental agencies. Positive contributions of varying scales can be made by diverse private or civil society agencies bringing their own resources to bear and working independently. The potential of such initiatives is enhanced when agencies working in the same field operate in such a way as to ensure that they do not directly compete with, duplicate or disrupt the activities of other agencies	• Community development approaches enacted by in-country sport and development NGOs • International civil society support for the development of sport facilities or initiatives, especially where government has identified gaps in existing provision

Just Play: Enhancing the contribution of sport to the 2030 Agenda for Sustainable Development

Evidence shows that 49 per cent of school-aged children in the Pacific region are overweight or obese by 13 years of age, and only 29 per cent participate in regular physical education classes. Meanwhile, children with disabilities often experience barriers to wide acceptance, and girls can be marginalised in education, decision-making and access to health services. Around 80 per cent of children have experienced some form of direct violence or abuse.

Just Play, delivered by the Oceania Football Confederation with the support of government partners and donor agencies, recognises the important role sport can play in supporting children's holistic development.

Targeting girls and boys, children with and without disabilities and children living in urban and rural communities, Just Play is a critical entry point to engage children aged 6-16 years in a positive and meaningful way. Children learn through active participation by means of social messages on health and wellness, gender equality, social inclusion and child protection.

Using a holistic approach and engagement with multiple stakeholders, Just Play is contributing to the achievement of four of the SDGs.

SDG 3: Health and Well-being: Children are motivated to learn to associate physical activity with fun. This positive association makes them more likely to continue to engage in some form of recreation throughout their lives. Just Play sessions also help children choose healthier food options. Together, these interventions contribute to SDG target 3.4 aimed at reducing premature mortality from non-communicable disease.

Over 90 per cent of children in the programme say sport makes them happy and they want to continue participating. Over two-thirds eat two fruit and three vegetable servings a day.

SDG 4: Quality Education: Just Play sessions enhance Ministry of Education learning outcomes. Children learn to develop healthy lifestyle habits, respect each other, understand the importance of handwashing and safe drinking water, support the inclusion of everyone, and keep themselves and their friends safe.

Eighty per cent of participants acknowledge and celebrate their differences. A total of 4,034 teachers and community members have improved capacity to deliver quality sports sessions, enhancing the quality of the education environment and relevance of the learning outcomes for all children, the focus of SDG target 4.1.

SDG 5: Gender Equality: Just Play promotes girls and boys to engage as one team. Girls and boys learn to respect each other and develop tolerance and understanding, which will be crucial in achieving SDG target 5.1, which aims to end all forms of discrimination against all women and girls everywhere. Just Play also promotes the development of female role models and offers girls and women the ability to acquire skills, in order to help them make a meaningful contribution to their communities.

Seventy per cent of boys say that they enjoying playing football with girls, and 95 per cent recognise that girls can play football. Eighty-nine per cent of children say that they enjoy having a female coach.

(Continued)

Just Play: Enhancing the contribution of sport to the 2030 Agenda for Sustainable Development (*cont.*)

SDG 17: Partnerships for the Goals: Working directly with government ministries and key stakeholders, such as ministries of education, ensures wider reach and programme scalability. Cross-cutting partnerships support the upskilling of teachers and community volunteers to ensure quality sporting interventions in and out of school. Through engagement with teachers and schools during class time, Just Play supports the delivery of a 16-week programme. The 34-week community based programme is delivered after schools with the support of community based stakeholders.

The programme's multi-sectoral approach (across health and wellness, gender, social inclusion and child protection) engages actors at the local, regional and country levels. The partnerships central to Just Play contribute to SDG target 17.9, focused on capacity building, SDG target 17.4 on policy coherence, and SDG targets 17.16 and 17.7 on multi-stakeholder partnerships.

The programme has had impacts on 238,478 children in 11 Pacific countries since its inception in 2009; 43 per cent of child participants are girls and 54 per cent of the teachers and community volunteers supporting the programme are women.

For more information on the programme please visit: www.justplayofc.org

3.4 Concluding implications for policy-makers

The four identified approaches are sufficiently flexible to encompass and enable cross-sectoral relationships and initiatives, as well as those that encourage collective implementation within the sport sector.

The framework indicates that relationships may be configured in different ways to enable collective implementation and development. The four identified approaches are sufficiently flexible to encompass and enable cross-sectoral relationships and initiatives, as well as those that encourage collective implementation within the sport sector. This flexibility also enables alignment between the framework and the use of different policy instruments, including the distribution and re-distribution of funding, the setting and enforcement of regulation, and the collation and distribution of various forms of information.

Furthermore, the different approaches within the framework are not mutually exclusive. There is a strong likelihood that specific public, private and civil society organisations will contribute within different approaches to collective implementation concurrently. For example, international NGOs may operate autonomously in some working environments and in complementary or structured relationships in others. Similarly, relationships between public, private and civil society organisations can be fluid and subject to change, and in so doing can develop across different approaches to collective implementation over time.

Policy-makers must also be particularly mindful of the levels of capacity required to pursue different approaches to collective implementation. Similarly, recognition of the scale of intervention required to work towards particular policy goals is a further relevant consideration. Above all, these factors point to the importance of employing the approaches to collective implementation that are most relevant to the specific contexts and policy goals to which they are directed. The need for the means of implementation to be tailored according to context-specific analysis of development needs and possibilities will inform the subsequent application of this four-fold framework across each of the specific SDGs considered in the chapters that follow.

References

Black, D. R. (2010), 'The ambiguities of development: implications for development through sport', *Sport in Society*, Vol. 13, 121–129.

Coalter, F. (2010), 'The politics of sport-for-development: Limited focus programmes and broad gauge problems?' *International Review for the Sociology of Sport*, Vol. 45, 295–314.

Cronin, Ó. (2011), *Comic Relief Review: Mapping the Research on the Impact of Sport and Development Interventions*, Orla Cronin Research, Manchester, available at: http://www.sportanddev.org/en/connect/userprofile.cfm?3096/Comic-Relief-Research-Mapping

Darnell, S. (2014), 'Critical Considerations for Sport for Development and Peace Policy Development', in Dudfield, O. (Ed.), *Strengthening Sport for Development and Peace: National Policies and Strategies*, Commonwealth Secretariat, London.

Darnell, S. C. and R. Huish (2015), 'Cuban sport policy and South-South development cooperation: an overview and analysis of the Escuela Internacional de Educación Física y Deporte, *International Journal of Sport Policy and Politics*, Vol. 7, 123–140.

Department of Sport and Recreation South Africa (2011), *National Sport and Recreation Plan*, available at: http://www.srsa.gov.za/MediaLib/Home/DocumentLibrary/Nasional%20Sport%20and%20Recretion%20Plan%20-%20Draft%2020.pdf

Dudfield, O. (2014), 'Sport for Development and Peace: Opportunities, Challenges and the Commonwealth's Response', in Dudfield, O. (Ed.), *Strengthening Sport for Development and Peace: National Policies and Strategies*, Commonwealth Secretariat, London.

Giulianotti, R. (2011a), 'The sport, development and peace sector: a model of four social policy domains', *Journal of Social Policy*, 40 issue 4, 757–76.

Giulianotti, R. (2011b), 'Sport, transnational peacemaking and global civil society: exploring the reflective discourses of "Sport, Development, and Peace" project officials', *Journal of Sport and Social Issues*, Vol. 35, 50–71.

Giulianotti, R. (2014), 'Sport for Development and Peace Policy Options in the Commonwealth', in Dudfield, O. (Ed.), *Strengthening Sport for Development and Peace. National Policies and Strategies*, Commonwealth Secretariat, London.

Hasselgård, A. and S. Straume (2015), 'Sport for development and peace policy discourse and local practice', *International Journal of Sport Policy and Politics*, Vol. 7, 87–103.

Hayhurst, L. M. C. and W. Frisby (2010), 'Inevitable tensions: Swiss and Canadian Sport for Development NGO perspectives on partnerships with high-performance sport', *European Sport Management Quarterly*, Vol. 10, 75–96.

Kay, T. (2012), 'Accounting for legacy: Monitoring and evaluation in sport in development relationships', *Sport in Society*, Vol. 15, 888–904.

Kay, T. and O. Dudfield (2013), *The Commonwealth Guide to Advancing Development through Sport*, Commonwealth Secretariat, London, available at: http://assets.thecommonwealth.org/assetbank-commonwealth/action/viewAsset?id=23162andindex=3andtotal=11andview=viewSearchItem

Keim, M. and C. de Coning (Eds) (2014), *Sport and Development Policy in Africa: Results of a Collaborative Study of Selected Country Cases*, SUN Press, Stellenbosch.

Kidd, B. (2008), 'A new social movement: Sport for Development and Peace', *Sport in Society*, Vol. 11, 370–380.

Kidd, B. (2011), 'Cautions, questions and opportunities in Sport for Development and Peace', *Third World Quarterly*, Vol. 32, 603–609.

Lindsey, I. (2016), 'Governance in Sport-for-Development: Problems and possibilities of (not) learning from international development', *International Review for the Sociology of Sport*, available at: http://irs.sagepub.com/content/early/2016/01/05/1012690215623460.abstract

Lindsey, I. and D. Banda (2011), 'Sport and the fight against HIV/AIDS in Zambia: A "partnership" approach?', *International Review of Sociology of Sport*, Vol. 46, 90–107.

Nicholson, M., R. Hoye and B. Houlihan (Eds) (2010), *Participation in Sport: International Policy Perspectives*, Routledge, Abingdon.

Sanders, B., J. Phillips and B Vanreusel. (2014), 'Opportunities and challenges facing NGOs using sport as a vehicle for development in post-apartheid South Africa' *Sport, Education and Society*, Vol. 19, 789–805.

Schulenkorf, N., E. Sherry and K. Rowe (2016), 'Sport for Development: An integrated literature review', *Journal of Sport Management*, Vol. 30, 22–39.

Sen, A. (Ed.) (2011), *Peace and Democratic Society*. Open Book Publishers / Commonwealth Secretariat, London.

Sport for Development and Peace International Working Group (SDPIWG) (2008), *Harnessing the Power of Sport for Development and Peace: Recommendations to Governments*, available at: http://www.un.org/wcm/content/site/sport/home/unplayers/memberstates/sdpiwg_keydocs

Wright, P. M., J. M. Jacobs, J. D. Ressler and J. Jung (2016), 'Teaching for transformative educational experience in a sport for development program', *Sport, Education and Society*, Vol. 21, 531–548.

Chapter 4 Measuring Progress: Data, Monitoring and Accountability (SDG 17)

4.1 Introduction

The scale and scope of the 17 SDGs and the 167 related targets is ambitious. Identifying whether or not these targets have been met by 2030 is, in itself, an ambitious objective, but one that is strongly prioritised in the *2030 Agenda for Sustainable Development*. Extensive work has been undertaken by the United Nations' Statistical Commission and a specific Inter-agency and Expert Group to develop a Global Indicator Framework for reviewing progress towards the SDGs. The Global Indicator Framework proposed in March 2016 consists of a total of 230 indicators across all SDGs and related targets (UNESCO 2016).

Extensive work has been undertaken by the United Nations' Statistical Commission and a specific Inter-agency and Expert Group to develop a Global Indicator Framework for reviewing progress towards the SDGs.

The assessment of levels of achievement against the Global Indicator Framework will be undertaken under the auspices of the United Nations General Assembly and the Economic and Social Council. While this process will draw on comparative data collected at national level, the *2030 Agenda for Sustainable Development* also places significant emphasis on the importance of country-led review processes and the development of complementary indicators relevant to national priorities and levels of development.

This guide and chapter focuses on this at national level in considering how different sources of data can be drawn upon to determine the contribution of sport to the SDGs. Various stakeholders have previously sought to respond to well-recognised limitations of the evidence-base for sport-based approaches. However, this remains a significant undertaking given the malleable and diverse ways in which sport has been utilised to address a wide range of development outcomes. Disparities remain in the breadth of the evidence-base that can be identified globally, nationally and with respect to particular initiatives. Of particular relevance to this guide are limitations in the collation and use of evidence for sport that can inform national-level policy development and implementation (Nicholson *et al.* 2010; Keim and de Coning 2014).

In this chapter, analysis of existing data collection and measures of progress for sport-based approaches will be followed by examination of how policy-makers could approach the task of evidencing the contribution of sport to the SDGs.

In this regard, there is ongoing recognition that reviewing progress towards the *2030 Agenda for Sustainable Development* will require 'capacity-building support for developing countries, including the strengthening of national data systems and evaluation programmes' (UNGA 2015). This requirement is specifically captured in SDG targets 17.18 and 17.19. In this chapter, analysis of existing data collection and measures of progress for sport-based approaches will be followed by examination of how policy-makers could approach the task of evidencing the contribution of sport to the SDGs.

4.2 Analysis of sport and specific SDG targets

Target 17.18 By 2020, enhance capacity-building support to developing countries, including for least developed countries and small island developing states, to increase significantly the availability of high-quality, timely and reliable data disaggregated by income, gender, age, race, ethnicity, migratory status, disability, geographic location and other characteristics relevant in national contexts.

Target 17.19 By 2030, build on existing initiatives to develop measurements of progress on sustainable development that complement gross domestic product, and support statistical capacity-building in developing countries.

The importance accorded to developing the evidence-base for sport-based approaches partly responds to concerns that inflated claims have been made for their impact (Coakley 2011). Such claims may fail to fully account for the magnitude of development challenges and the complexity of identifying the contribution of particular sport-based initiatives (Coalter 2010). However, recognition of the scope and limitations of evidence for sport-based approaches has been significantly enhanced through different reviews, including those that have been commissioned by organisations, such as the Sport for Development and Peace International Working Group, and others that have been undertaken independently (SDPIWG 2008; Cronin 2011; Schulenkorf *et al.* 2016). Commonly, such reviews have reached nuanced and carefully qualified conclusions regarding the potential of sport to contribute to development outcomes.

Significant efforts and resources have also been assigned to capacity-building to improve evidence generation with respect to sport-based approaches (Levermore 2011). Guidelines and toolkits which have been designed to support the monitoring and evaluation of sport-based approaches reflect the prioritisation, to date, of evidencing the impact of specific initiatives (see, for example, Burnett and Uys 2000; Coalter 2006; sportcoachUK 2011). Concerns have been raised that this prioritisation may be representative of accountability systems that are primarily oriented towards external donors (Kay 2012). Especially with there being recognised limitations as regards the scale and quality of evidence for sport-based approaches in developing countries (Lindsey *et al.* 2016), further effort is required to ensure that context-relevant knowledge effectively informs policies and practices for sport and development.

Guidelines and toolkits which have been designed to support the monitoring and evaluation of sport-based approaches reflect the prioritisation, to date, of evidencing the impact of specific initiatives.

Levels of data availability vary from country to country, and many do not have well-established or rigorously implemented national systems of data collection specific to sport (Nicholson *et al.* 2010; Keim and de Coning 2014). More generalised data from official national statistics are unlikely, in isolation, to provide sufficient understanding of the way that sport-based approaches may contribute to particular SDG targets and indicators. Nevertheless, a range of evidence sources may be available to national policy-makers in order to make reasoned judgements on the contribution of sport towards the SDGs (see Figure 4.1). There are several levels of evidence that may be considered to help make such judgements, including:

- **national and international level data** – such as official statistics on the economy, health, education and the labour market, some of which may have particular indicators relevant to sport
- **regional- and local-level data** – such as disaggregated census data and official statistics, and data generated to monitor public-sector initiatives driven by local policy
- **evidence drawn from monitoring and evaluation of discrete initiatives** – such as the monitoring and evaluation of international, national or locally based sport-based initiatives, undertaken by civil society or private sector organisations

Figure 4.1 Measuring progress

Source: United Nations Economic and Social Comm ssion

- **evidence from academic research** – findings which may have been collected in discrete spatial locations, or specific disciplinary or thematic foci and can therefore provide evidence upon which, for example, policy decisions for the scaling-up of sport-based approaches can be reasonably made.

In considering the use of such evidence, recognition must be given to how sport-based approaches may make direct or indirect contributions in relation to particular SDGs, targets and indicators. A direct contribution may be defined and identified where a sport-based approach has an identifiable impact, independent of other factors, by, for example, making a discrete economic contribution to gross domestic product (GDP) through sport tourism, or by making a direct contribution to the achievement of equal opportunities for women through specific employment practices. An indirect contribution may be achieved alongside other activities beyond the realm of sport. In such circumstances, determining that sport has made a tangible contribution may require the collation of contributory evidence towards a stated goal. Examples may include the use of evidence on the contribution of sport-based activities to specific aspects of public health education. Table 4.1 (overleaf) provides examples of how sport-based approaches may contribute directly or

Recognition must be given to how sport-based approaches may make direct or indirect contributions in relation to particular SDGs, targets and indicators.

Table 4.1 Examples of direct or indirect contributions towards SDGs, specific targets and indicators

SDGs and exemplar targets	UN agreed indicators	Potential/indicative evidence for direct and indirect contribution of sport towards targets and indicators
SDG 3: Ensure healthy lives and promote well-being for all, at all ages		
Target 3.4 By 2030, reduce by one-third premature mortality from non-communicable diseases through prevention and treatment, and promote mental health and well-being	3.4.1 Mortality of cardiovascular disease, cancer, diabetes or chronic respiratory disease	*Direct:* National or local data identifying the contribution of sport participation to increased physical activity among particular population groups, correlated with WHO physical activity guidelines *Indirect:* Evaluation that indicates the contribution of sport-based education to increased awareness of health and physical inactivity issues

(Continued)

Table 4.1 Examples of direct or indirect contributions towards SDGs, specific targets and indicators (*cont.*)

SDGs and exemplar targets	UN agreed indicators	Potential/indicative evidence for direct and indirect contribution of sport towards targets and indicators
SDG 4: Ensure inclusive and equitable quality education and promote lifelong learning opportunities for all		
Target 4.5 By 2030, eliminate gender disparities in education and ensure equal access to all levels of education and vocational training for the vulnerable, including persons with disabilities, indigenous peoples and children in vulnerable situations	4.5.1 Parity indices (female/male, rural/urban, bottom/top wealth quintile and others such as disability status, indigenous peoples and conflict-affected as data become available) for all [SDG 4] indicators that can be disaggregated	*Direct*: Evaluation of targeted sport-based approaches that indicate their impact on enabling females (or otherwise vulnerable persons) to engage in education or other forms of vocational training *Indirect*: National or local data of participation in physical education and sport in educational settings that are disaggregated by gender and other parity indices
SDG 5: Achieve gender equality and empower all women and girls		
Target 5.1: End all forms of discrimination against all women and girls everywhere	5.1.1 Whether or not legal frameworks are in place to promote, enforce and monitor equality and non-discrimination on the basis of sex	*Direct*: National data that disaggregate participation in sport by sex to monitor progress towards ending inequality and discrimination *Indirect*: Academic research that may indicate the cultural and material effects of the institution of policy and legal frameworks on discrimination in sport
SDG 8: Promote sustained, inclusive and sustainable economic growth, full and productive employment and decent work for all		
Target 8.1 Sustain per capita economic growth in accordance with national circumstances and, in particular, at least 7% GDP growth per annum in the least developed countries	8.1.1 Annual growth rate of real GDP per capita	*Direct*: National and local data that disaggregate the contribution of sport-based activity to GDP *Indirect*: Academic research that can be used to estimate the economic impact of particular strategies to lever economic impact via, for example, sport-related tourism

(*Continued*)

Table 4.1 Examples of direct or indirect contributions towards SDGs, specific targets and indicators (*cont.*)

SDGs and exemplar targets	UN agreed indicators	Potential/indicative evidence for direct and indirect contribution of sport towards targets and indicators
SDG 11: Make cities and human settlements inclusive, safe, resilient and sustainable		
Target 11.7 By 2030, provide universal access to safe, inclusive and accessible green and public spaces, in particular for women and children, older persons and persons with disabilities	11.7.1 The average share of the built-up area of cities that is open space for public use for all, disaggregated by age group, sex and persons with disabilities	*Direct*: Monitoring/evaluation data for specific or multiple facilities that indicate usage by age group, sex and persons with disabilities, disaggregated by locality *Indirect*: Local planning data on urban space available for sport and active recreation use
SDG 16: Promote peaceful and inclusive societies for sustainable development, provide access to justice for all, and build effective, accountable and inclusive institutions at all levels		
Target 16.5 Substantially reduce corruption and bribery in all their forms	16.5.1 Percentage of persons who had at least one contact with a public official, who paid a bribe to a public official, or were asked for a bribe by these public officials, in the previous 12 months, disaggregated by age group, sex, region and population group	*Direct*: National monitoring data on cases of corruption identified in sport *Indirect*: Monitoring/evaluation on indicators of good governance within sporting federations and other bodies

indirectly towards SDG targets and specific indicators. These are presented here for illustrative purposes, and further analysis is provided throughout the remainder of this guide.

The preceding analysis indicates the constraints and possibilities in respect of the availability of data and evidence on sport-based approaches. The next section identifies how available data may be used and analysed to assess the contribution of sport-based approaches to sustainable development.

4.3 Methods for measuring and assessing the impact of sport-based approaches

Claims regarding the direct or indirect contribution of sport-based approaches to SDG targets need to give due care and attention to the way that definitions of value are constructed and how sources of data are interpreted to indicate positive contributions. Whether considering individual SDG indicators that are specified in different ways or seeking to measure and assess particular sport-based approaches, a number of terms can be used to distinguish between different sources of 'value':

- ***The value of outputs*** – this is usually a measure of the value of the productivity of the intervention. Often it is possible to enumerate this value, i.e. the number of people who participated in a sport-based initiative, or who engaged in specific education activities, or who fulfilled particular leadership roles. Such measures indicate the level of *productivity* of a project, but do not necessarily indicate its *social, economic or environmental value.*

- ***The value of outcomes*** – outcomes can be defined as changes in people's lives, the economy or the environment that have been achieved as a direct result of an activity associated with particular institutional policies, interventions or initiatives.

- ***The value of impact*** – impact can be defined as the identification of a tangible effect that wholly or partly meets wider strategic goals. This is more difficult to measure because initiatives and interventions generally occur in the context of many other indirect influences.

There are several examples of evaluation frameworks which refer to outputs, outcomes and impact (see, for example, Barker and Watson 2010; Rickey and Olgain 2011; Parsons *et al.* 2013).

It is generally not possible to isolate contributory factors with sufficient dexterity to provide 'proof' of the direct impact of sport-based approaches.

With the exception of a limited number of areas of experimental sport science research (in fields such as physiology), it is generally not possible to isolate contributory factors with sufficient dexterity to provide 'proof' of the direct impact of sport-based approaches. Making effective judgements, at national level, on the contribution of a range of government-led, partnership, complementary or autonomous sport-based approaches may therefore require 'triangulation' of different sources of evidence (Murray 2016). Different types of approaches to triangulation can be adopted, with potentially varying implications and uses for policy-making. Furthermore, as indicated by the following three exemplar types of approaches, each may utilise and require different forms of existing data and evidence (Denzin 2002; Greene 2007; Howe 2010; Fielding 2012):

- ***Triangulation of findings from complementary studies using a range of methodologies*** – where findings are drawn from a mix of quantitative studies (produced by experimental methods, survey methods and demographic data analysis) and qualitative studies (using methods such as interviews and observation) to make evidence-based judgements on likely associations between features of specific interventions and their consequences.
- ***Triangulation of evidence from studies using the same or similar methods of data collection*** – such an approach allows for comparative assessments (by, for example, specific geographical areas, population characteristics or points in time) and meta-analytical review techniques, particularly in the field of health research, to assess results from a broad range of studies in order to determine generalised findings regarding the effects of interventions or initiatives.
- ***Theory-driven triangulation*** – the purpose of such an approach is to compare the conclusions drawn from research which has been undertaken from different positions of theoretical interest or political/conceptual standpoints. Such approaches can be used to undertake 'gap analyses' of specific areas of exploration that may have been previously overlooked or that are of specific interest for policy and practice.

The process of data triangulation, as indicated above, may involve drawing upon a range of theoretical ideas, official statistics and empirical evidence to make credible judgements on the direct or indirect effect of sport-based activity towards a particular social, economic or environmental objective. Sources of evidence may range from those collected through conventional approaches to scientific enquiry (Hilgartner *et al.*

2008; Jasanoff 2004), to studies which claim to determine the social return on investment in sports-based activity (Cabinet Office 2009; Fujiwara *et al.* 2014; Davies *et al.* 2016). Ideally, such work would be undertaken from the outset of a policy intervention or initiative by adopting mixed-method approaches to enquiry; however, it may alternatively be undertaken by retrospective reappraisal of many sources of evidence.

Approaches to evaluation and triangulation are generally underpinned by principles which require the identification of actual or potential patterns that indicate the contributions of policy interventions or initiatives to positive change.

Approaches to evaluation and triangulation are generally underpinned by principles which require the identification of actual or potential patterns that indicate the contributions of policy interventions or initiatives to positive change. Such analysis requires that the relative importance of a range of variables or factors are ordered collectively and/or sequentially to measure desired economic, social or environmental impacts. Policy-makers' growing interest in the identification of tangible evidence for the contribution of specific interventions to positive change has led to the development of pragmatic methodological approaches to show the extent of impact and the patterns of influences that contribute to it. For example, the current popularity of 'theory of change' models can be appealing to policy-makers because of their strong focus on the 'end point' of interventions in impact terms; for such models, evidence is garnered to show what additional benefit has been 'produced' from investment in interventions and initiatives to achieve social, economic and/or environmental change.

Using this approach, analysts begin by assembling a range of factors in causal chains which demonstrate how an intervention may contribute to or detract from the achievement of a desired outcome. Such factors may include, for example, the biographical characteristics of participants (for example, age, sex, ethnicity, race, disability, educational achievement and socio-economic status) so that it is possible to examine the extent to which an initiative produces the desired outputs, outcomes and impact for specific groups. Further specific evaluations of sport-based approaches have, for example, sought empirical evidence of identifiable and positive contributions to behavioural change which, in turn, may contribute towards particular public health outcomes (Coalter 2013). In other analyses, the presumed benefit of an intervention may be 'monetised'. Cost-benefit or social return on investment analysis has, for example, attempted to show how much money governments may subsequently save, or how much social value is produced, by investing in preventive measures. Increasing numbers of examples are available of such approaches being applied to sport. There has been a number of attempts to claim significant long-term benefit from sport initiatives through cost-benefit analysis and social return on investment (SROI) (see, for example, Crabbe 2013; ICF/GHK 2013; Davies *et al.* 2016).

Attempts to justify specific sport-based contributions to public health could result in attention and resources being detracted from other forms of physical activity that may have the potential to engage sections of the population for whom sport is unattractive.

The use of the available methodological approaches to explain relationships between contributory factors can be controversial if claims about the attribution of benefit from interventions are difficult to directly discern or appear to be exaggerated in some way. The risk of over-claiming the impact of interventions can be increased when impact indicators are based on predictions of what 'might' have happened if the intervention had not taken place. For example, in respect of sport-based initiatives that aim to help young people who are assessed as being 'at risk' of criminality, spurious associations may be made about the statistical likelihood of individuals committing a criminal act had they not taken part; furthermore, such approaches to analysis can reinforce negative stereotypes and encourage the assimilation of deficit models of certain categories of young people (Darnell 2012; Chapman, *et al.* 2015). Controversies can also emerge when approaches to defining positive impact are underpinned by funding imperatives which may meet the interests of one constituency of beneficiaries, but do so at the expense of others (see, for example, Nutley and Davies 2002; Packwood 2002; Tenbensel 2004; Laforest and Orsini 2005). For example, attempts to justify specific sport-based contributions to public health could result in attention and resources being detracted from other forms of physical activity that may have the potential to engage sections of the population for whom sport is unattractive. This example reinforces the potential benefit of seeking more collective approaches not only to implementation, but also to evaluation and reviewing progress.

4.4 Concluding implications for policy-makers

Reliable and evidence-based judgements on progress towards the SDGs are vital to inform policy at global, national and sub-national levels but, as this chapter has shown, the production of reliable indicators of impact can be hard to come by and evidence of social, economic or environmental impact can be subject to a range of interpretations. Furthermore, the importance given in the *2030 Agenda for Sustainable Development* to reviewing

Sport for Development Shared Measurement Framework

United Kingdom

Emma Heel
Head of Evidence and Learning
Sported

The physical health benefits of sport are widely understood, but can sport really reduce anti-social behaviour or raise employment levels? Does it have the power to influence people's social and emotional capacities or improve community relations?

That is the challenge facing many organisations, which, through the intentional use of sport or physical activity, are working to improve the lives of individuals, communities or society as a whole. Those working in this area know they are making a difference, and fully believe in the power of sport as a viable, cost-effective solution – when it's done well.

Although different organisations have different priorities, there is value in sport-for-development stakeholders using a common language when talking about outcomes and a common approach to measurement. If these stakeholders want to strengthen practice, they need to be able to engage in meaningful and useful conversations about 'what works' to improve programme design and delivery.

This was the driving force behind the creation of a Shared Measurement Framework, developed by the United Kingdom's Sport for Development Coalition and informed by consultation with sport for development organisations, academics and industry experts in the country. Critically, the Sport for Development Coalition worked closely with the United Kingdom Government Department for Culture, Media and Sport, and the National Sport Council (Sport England) to align our Framework with the government strategy 'Sporting Future: A New Strategy for an Active Nation', released in December 2015.

A joined-up approach to measuring progress sends a strong message to stakeholders in other policy areas that the use of sport as a tool to improve the lives of individuals and communities should be taken seriously.

Sport for development outcomes can be either intrinsic or extrinsic. For example, a programme can support young people to increase their self-esteem and manage their emotions, and also to develop extrinsic behaviours, such as being active and healthy, learning and having a job. Outcomes can change individual emotional skills and behaviours and as a result influence family lives, communities and wider society.

To capture the range of outcomes that sport for development programmes deliver, we mapped these two continuums against each other to create a Sport for Development Outcomes Model.

The model identifies four distinct groups of outcomes:

1. social, emotional and cognitive capabilities
2. individual achievements and behaviours
3. interpersonal relationships
4. benefits to society.

(Continued)

Sport for Development Shared Measurement Framework (*cont.*)

The model suggests that there are potential links between all four groups of outcomes. These are not direct casual links between each outcome group: they are based on the limited evidence available and represent the Sport for Development Coalition's hypothesis that sport for development can cause positive changes in a wide range of outcomes.

Ultimately, the Shared Measurement Framework is designed to empower providers and funders, encouraging them to take responsibility for better understanding their work and providing evidence on how they are contributing. It also directly responds to SDG targets 17.18 and 17.19 that call for an increase in 'quality, timely and reliable disaggregated data...to enable a more robust measurement of progress on sustainable development'.

The Sport for Development Coalition is continuing to consult, test and improve the current Framework. Sported in particular is focused on how we can make the Framework accessible, useable and useful for grassroots sport for development organisations in the United Kingdom, who are making a difference to young people and communities but often find it tough to prove it.

---

progress based on country priorities, processes and indicators has particular implications for sport. Assessing the contribution of sport to sustainable development needs to be initially framed by questions about what may be achievable given, for example, the current status of development in respect of particular SDGs, and also the scale of available investment. Consideration must also be given to whether, and which particular, contributions of sport may be plausibly identifiable through the collection, analysis and collation of appropriate evidence.

Care and realism must be applied to any judgements regarding the specific contribution of sport-based approaches and policies.

Diverse sport-based approaches associated with government-led, structured partnerships, complementary and autonomous implementation and involving various organisations may directly or indirectly contribute to, and provide evidence of, positive change. In addition, contributions to positive change do not often come solely from sport but arise in association and alongside those made in other sectors, such as education, health and economic development. Furthermore, progress towards SDGs may not always be a linear process, so care and realism must be applied to any judgements regarding the specific contribution of sport-based approaches and policies. Countries' progress towards the achievement of SDG targets may, for example, be affected by a range of factors, including significant global economic shifts, environmental factors, significant social upheaval or conflict, which may be largely beyond the control of governments or other stakeholders.

There remains a need for significant capacity-building and further dedicated investment if effective approaches to measuring and reviewing progress are to be widely adopted and utilised in different country contexts.

Nevertheless, judgements about the contribution of sport-based approaches can still usefully be made by drawing upon a range of sources of data and evidence where available. Specific methodologies which are adopted to evaluate discrete areas of policy and practice, together with attempts to triangulate a wider range of sources of evidence, can help support policy-makers in the process of making balanced and reasonable assessments of progress. Choices regarding particular approaches and methodologies may depend on a number of factors, and the scale and type of existing data and evidence may also enable or preclude particular approaches. To enable more rigorous processes of triangulation, sport and development organisations and other researchers should be encouraged to make their data and findings widely available. Furthermore, the extent to which different methodological approaches encompass analysis of contextual influences varies. Consideration of the particularities of local contexts and of national development priorities has been recommended as a priority for evaluation and research design, particularly where undertaken by international sport and development organisations or researchers (Kay 2012). Finally, while several methodologies for evaluation and triangulation have become available and are increasingly being used by sport and development organisations (Harris and Adams 2015), the distribution of resources to undertake such work is uneven in respect of different countries and in different areas of provision. Therefore, there remains a need for significant capacity-building and further dedicated investment if effective approaches to measuring and reviewing progress are to be widely adopted and utilised in different country contexts.

References

Barker, Y. and A. Watson (2010), *Measuring the Contribution of Culture and Sport to Outcomes*, Improvement and Development Association, London.

Burnett, C. and T. Uys (2000), 'Sport development impact assessment: towards a rationale and tool', *South African Journal for Research in Sport, Physical Education and Recreation*, Vol. 22, 27–40.

Cabinet Office (2009), *A Guide to Social Return on Investment*, Cabinet Office, London.

Chapman, T., S. Rich, H. Wilson and A. Crowther (2015), *Evaluation of the National Youth Agency Social Action Journey Fund Programme*, available at: http://www.stchads.ac.uk/wp-content/uploads/2015/09/SAJF-NYA-PROJECT-EVALUATION-REPORT-FINAL-25th-June1.pdf

Coakley, J. (2011), 'Youth sports: What counts as "positive development"?', *Journal of Sport and Social Issues*, Vol. 35, 306–324.

Coalter, F. (2006), *Sport-in-Development: A Monitoring and Evaluation Manual*, available at: http://assets.sportanddev.org/downloads/10__sport_in_development__a_monitoring_and_evaluation_manual.pdf

Coalter, F. (2010), 'The politics of sport-for-development: Limited focus programmes and broad gauge problems?' *International Review for the Sociology of Sport*, Vol. 45, 295–314.

Coalter, F. (2013), *Sport for Development: What Game are We Playing?* Routledge, Abingdon.

Crabbe, T. (2013), *Sportworks. Investing in Sport for Development and Creating the Business Case to Help Change the Lives of Disadvantaged Young People in the UK*, available at: http://www.substance.net/wp-content/uploads/2015/01/Sportworks-Full-Report.pdf

Cronin, Ó. (2011), *Comic Relief Review: Mapping the Research on the Impact of Sport and Development Interventions*, Orla Cronin Research, Manchester, available at: http://www.sportanddev.org/en/connect/userprofile.cfm?3096/Comic-Relief-Research-Mapping

Darnell, S. (2012), *Sport for Development and Peace: A Critical Sociology*, Bloomsbury Academic, London.

Davies, L., P. Taylor, G. Ramchandani and E. Christy (2016), *Social Return on Investment in Sport: A Participation-wide Model for England*, available at: https://www.sportanddev.org/sites/default/files/downloads/sroi_england_report.pdf

Denzin, N. K. (2002), 'Triangulation 2.0*', *Journal of Mixed Methods Research*, Vol. 6, 80–88.

Fielding, N. G. (2012), 'Triangulation and mixed methods designs: data integration with new research technologies', *Journal of Mixed Methods Research*, Vol. 6, 89–96.

Fujiwara, D., L. Kudrna and P. Dolan (2014), *Quantifying and Valuing the Well-being Impacts of Culture and Sport*, available at: https://www.gov.uk/government/uploads/system/uploads/attachment_data/file/304899/Quantifying_and_valuing_the_well-being_impacts_of_sport_and_culture.pdf

Greene, J. C. (2007), *Mixed Methods in Social Inquiry*, Jossey-Bass, San Francisco.

Harris, K. and A. Adams (2015), 'Power and discourse in the politics of evidence in sport for development', *Sport Management Review*, Vol. 19, 97–106.

Hilgartner, S., N. Nelson and A. Geltzer (2008), 'The anticipatory state: Making policy-relevant knowledge about the future', *Science and Public Policy*, Vol. 8, 546–606.

Howe, K. R. (2010), 'Mixed methods, triangulation, and causal explanation', *Journal of Mixed Methods Research*, Vol. 6, 89–96.

ICF/GHK (2013), *Social Return on Investment Evaluation of the Sportivate Programme in the Black Country*, GHK Consulting, Birmingham.

Jasanoff, S. (2004), 'Ordering Knowledge, Ordering Society', in Jasanoff, S. (Ed.), *States of Knowledge: The Coproduction of Science and Social Order*, Routledge, London.

Kay, T. (2012), Accounting for legacy: Monitoring and evaluation in sport in development relationships, *Sport in Society*, Vol. 15, 888–904.

Keim, M. and C. de Coning (Eds) (2014), *Sport and Development Policy in Africa: Results of a Collaborative Study of Selected Country Cases*, SUN Press, Stellenbosch.

Laforest, R. and M. Orsini (2005), 'Evidence-based engagement in the voluntary sector: Lessons from Canada', *Social Policy and Administration*, Vol. 39, 481–497.

Levermore, R. (2011), 'Evaluating sport-for-development approaches and critical issues', *Progress in Development Studies*, Vol. 11, 339–353.

Lindsey, I., T. Kay, R. Jeanes and D. Banda. (2016), *Localizing Global Sport for Development*, Manchester University Press, Manchester.

Murray, S. (2016), 'Reflection on beyond girl power and the girl effect: The girling of Sport for Development and Peace', in Hayhurst, L. M. C., T. Kay and M. Chawansky (Eds), *Beyond Sport for Development and Peace: Transnational Perspectives on Theory, Policy and Practice*, Routledge, Abingdon, 106–110.

Nicholson, M., R. Hoye and B. Houlihan (Eds) (2010), *Participation in Sport: International Policy Perspectives*, Routledge, Abingdon.

Nutley, S. and H. Davies (2002), *Evidence-Based Policy and Practice: Cross Sector Lessons from the UK*, available at: https://www.kcl.ac.uk/sspp/departments/politicaleconomy/research/cep/pubs/papers/assets/wp9b.pdf

Packwood, A. (2002), 'Evidence-based policy: rhetoric and reality', *Social Policy and Society*, Vol. 1, 267–272.

Parsons, J., C. Gokey and M. Thornton (2013), *Indicators of Inputs, Activities, Outputs, Outcomes and Impact in Security and Justic Programmes*, Department for International Development, London.

Rickey, B. and E. Olgain (2011), *A Journey to Greater Impact*, New Philanthropy Capital, London.

Schulenkorf, N., E. Sherry and K. Rowe (2016), 'Sport for Development: An integrated literature review', *Journal of Sport Management*, Vol. 30, 22–39.

Sport for Development and Peace International Working Group (SDPIWG) (2008), *Harnessing the Power of Sport for Development and Peace: Recommendations to Governments*, available at: http://www.un.org/wcm/content/site/sport/home/unplayers/memberstates/sdpiwg_keydocs

sportcoachUK (2011), *Impact Measuring ToolKit*, available at: http://www.sportscoachuk.org/sites/default/files/ToolKit.pdf

Tenbensel, T. (2004), 'Does more evidence lead to better policy? The implications of explicit priority-setting in New Zealand's health policy for evidence-based policy', *Policy Studies*, Vol. 25, 180–207.

United Nations General Assembly (UNGA) (2015), *Transforming our World: The 2030 Agenda for Sustainable Development*, available at: www.un.org/ga/search/view_doc.asp?symbol=A/70/L.1andLang=E

UNESCO (2016), *Report of the Inter-Agency and Expert Group on Sustainable Development Goal Indicators*, available at: unstats.un.org/unsd/statcom/47th-session/documents/2016-2-IAEG-SDGs-E.pdf

Section Two

Sport and Sustainable Development

Chapter 5
Introduction to Sport and Sustainable Development

The chapters in Section Two consider each of the six SDGs that have been identified, through extensive consultation with Commonwealth stakeholders (Commonwealth Secretariat 2016), as those that sport may be well placed to make effective and cost-efficient contributions to. Each chapter follows the same structure: firstly, an overview of the particular SDG and pertinent considerations with regard to it is provided; then an evidenced analysis of how the contribution of sport to particular SDG targets may be enhanced is presented; and finally, based on the frameworks and approaches identified in Section One of this guide, potential policy options to enhance implementation that can strengthen the contribution of sport-based approaches towards the goal are offered.

Common considerations regarding sport-based approaches underpin and link all six chapters. These considerations are founded upon the understanding that sport-based approaches may influence and be influenced by social, economic and environmental elements of sustainable development at different levels, from the individual to the structural level. Across these levels, a summary of different elements relevant to sport-based approaches is shown in Table 5.1.

Sport-based approaches may influence and be influenced by social, economic and environmental elements of sustainable development at different levels, from the individual to the structural level.

The following six chapters relate to elements ranging from the individual to the structural levels, as identified in Table 5.1, in different measure. However, it is important to emphasise that the influence of, and impact on, different elements does not occur in isolation from other elements. Just as the SDGs are presented as 'integrated and indivisible', varied potential contributions of sport in respect of different goals and targets can be, and may need to be, mutually reinforcing. For example, enhancing the 'situational' provision of spaces and facilities (SDG 11) can be a vital factor in improving 'individual' health and well-being through participation in sport and active recreation (SDG 3).

Identifying these different levels and elements also draws attention to the varying scale and depth of the potential contributions of

Table 5.1 Elements relevant to sport-based approaches and sustainable development

Individual elements	Relational elements	Situational elements	Structural elements
Material well-being Individual attributes (intelligence, health and well-being) Skills and aptitudes (credentials, talents, attractiveness, etc.) Personality and temperament	Family and intimate relationships Peer and friendship networks Community and neighbourhood relationships Relationships in education and employment contexts	Local political, economic and environmental factors Local demography, culture and community safety, cohesion Local service provision, infrastructure and facilities	Social, cultural, and political and economic conditions Institutional structures (e.g. educational, legal, criminal justice systems) Economic and labour market conditions

Source: Adapted from Chapman *et al.* (2015)

sport-based approaches to particular SDGs. In the case of sport-based approaches which aim at improvements at the individual level, for example, depth refers to changes in people's lives which can be, for example, transformative and sustainably beneficial. Other sport-based approaches may seek to produce less radical change at the individual level, but produce change at a greater scale by, for example, producing positive outcomes for a more inclusive range of individuals. For example, structural changes to improve governance within sport organisations (SDG 16) may not have immediate impacts that are distinguishable at the individual level, but such changes are nevertheless important for underpinning the wider contribution of sport-based approaches across different forms of sustainable development.

Not only may different sport-based approaches seek to make contributions of varying scale and depth but, equally, these contributions will vary between individuals and different contexts. 'Starting points' towards the SDGs substantially differ between individuals in the same context, in respect of structural conditions in different countries, and also in terms of levels and elements in between these two ends of the spectrum. Consequently, it is important to recognise that policy developments that contribute to 'small steps' forward – for individuals, communities or countries that are disadvantaged or marginalised – can represent 'giant leaps' in material and cultural terms.

Policy developments that contribute to 'small steps' forward – for individuals, communities or countries that are disadvantaged or marginalised – can represent 'giant leaps' in material and cultural terms.

The analysis in the following six chapters recognises, where appropriate and feasible, the influence of context, and also the potential scale and depth of potential sport-based contributions to particular SDGs. Nevertheless, those utilising this guide are recommended to further appraise contextual conditions when deciding on policy priorities and implementation. Sport-based approaches have greatest potential when their use is differentiated according to in-depth analysis of individual, relational, situational and structural conditions (Kay and Dudfield 2013).

Sport-based approaches have greatest potential when their use is differentiated according to in-depth analysis of individual, relational, situational and structural conditions.

Such differentiation remains relevant in respect of the policy options presented in the final section of each chapter in Section Two. Policy options are identified in respect of the SDG 17 targets for country-leadership and policy coherence, mobilising financial and human resources, and country-specific and disaggregated 'measures of progress'. It is also recognised that the various policy options presented require different forms of government-led, structured partnership, complementary and autonomous implementation. Structuring policy options in this way allows for their implementation to be differentiated, but, again, policy-makers must still consider the specific application of proposed policy options within particular contexts.

References

Chapman, T. *et al.* (2015), *Evaluation of the National Youth Agency Social Action Journey Fund Programme*, available at: http://www.stchads.ac.uk/wp-content/uploads/2015/09/SAJF-NYA-PROJECT-EVALUATION-REPORT-FINAL-25th-June1.pdf

Commonwealth Secretariat (2016), *Sport for Development and Peace and the 2030 Agenda for Sustainable Development Analysis Report*. Commonwealth Secretariat, London.

Kay, T. and O. Dudfield (2013), *The Commonwealth Guide to Advancing Development through Sport*, Commonwealth Secretariat, London, available at: http://assets.thecommonwealth.org/assetbank-commonwealth/action/viewAsset?id=23162andindex=3andtotal=11andview=viewSearchItem

Chapter 6
Ensure Healthy Lives and Promote Well-being for All, at All Ages (SDG 3)

6.1 Introduction

Universal and holistic conceptions of health and well-being are at the forefront of the *2030 Agenda for Sustainable Development* and are collectively prioritised across the Commonwealth (Commonwealth Secretariat 2015). The paradigm shift from the more specific focus of the MDGs on child mortality, maternal health, HIV/AIDS, malaria and tuberculosis recognises the immense significance of global health threats that have risen to prominence in the interim. Non-communicable diseases now account for 38 million deaths per year, of which 28 million are in low- to medium-income countries (WHO 2015a). Mental illness is expected to account for 15 per cent of the global burden of disease by 2020, with young people disproportionately affected (Biddle and Asare 2011).

Policies that can contribute to increasing participation in sport and active recreation can reduce inactivity and, in so doing, significantly contribute to SDG target 3.4, which seeks to address non-communicable diseases and promote mental health and well-being.

Physical inactivity has become one of the most significant health issues of the twenty-first century. Inactivity is the fourth greatest risk factor for global mortality, causing approximately 3.2 million deaths per year (WHO 2010). Consistent international data indicate that inactivity directly accounts for between 1 and 4 per cent of all healthcare costs (Davis *et al.* 2014), with indirect consequences of physical inactivity for economic productivity being substantially higher (see Figure 6.1). Policies that can contribute to increasing participation in sport and active recreation can reduce inactivity and, in so doing, significantly contribute to SDG target 3.4, which seeks to address non-communicable diseases and promote mental health and well-being (see Box 6.1). Furthermore, there is now also a significant history of sport-based approaches being used as part of health promotion and education strategies. Enhancing and expanding those initiatives that are currently effective at contributing to the prevention of communicable diseases, including those associated with sexual health, and the reduction of drug and alcohol abuse, can support the achievement of SDG targets 3.3, 3.5 and 3.7.

Figure 6.1 Cost of physical inactivity

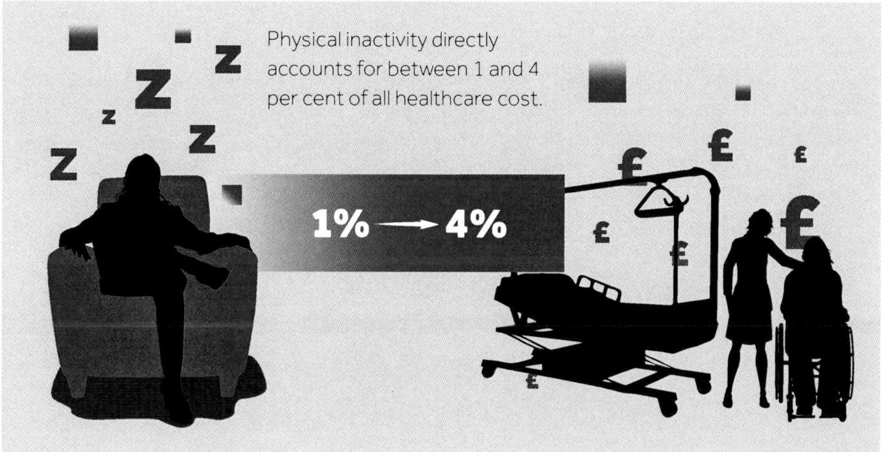

Source: Davis *et al.* (2014)

Box 6.1 Enhancing the contribution of sport to Sustainable Development Goal 3: Key policy implications

- Participation in sport and active recreation can make a substantial contribution to reducing physical inactivity, preventing associated non-communicable diseases, and improving health and well-being.
- Popular engagement with sport makes it a valuable environment for communication and education to address various health challenges and outcomes.
- Policies that enable the alignment and integration of sport-based approaches with multi-sectoral implementation strategies can leverage significant benefits for improved health and well-being.
- The collection of disaggregated data on engagement in sport and physical activity enables improved policy development, targeting of resources and well-designed initiatives.
- Sport-based approaches must be accessible and inclusive, taking into account and seeking to address wider social, economic and environmental factors that affect health and well-being.

6.2 Analysis of sport and specific SDG targets

Target 3.4 By 2030, reduce by one-third premature mortality from non-communicable diseases through prevention and treatment, and promote mental health and well-being.

Evidence clearly indicates that regular physical activity, including sport and active recreation, helps to address a variety of non-communicable diseases through contributing to the prevention of obesity, and the reduction of the risks of heart disease, stroke, diabetes and some forms of cancer. Young people can benefit from increased physical fitness, reduced body fat, positive cardiovascular and metabolic disease risk profiles, and enhanced bone health (WHO 2014b). The World Health Organization (WHO) produces clear guidelines for the recommended levels of physical activity for health across all age groups (WHO 2010) (see Box 6.2 and Figure 6.2).

Box 6.2 World Health Organization recommendations on physical activity for health

Children aged 5–17 years

1. Children and youth aged 5–17 should accumulate at least 60 minutes of moderate- to vigorous-intensity physical activity daily.
2. Amounts of physical activity greater than 60 minutes provide additional health benefits.
3. Most of the daily physical activity should be aerobic. Vigorous-intensity activities should be incorporated, including those that strengthen muscle and bone, at least three times per week.

Adults aged 18–64 years

1. Adults aged 18–64 should do at least 150 minutes of moderate-intensity aerobic physical activity throughout the week, or do at least 75 minutes of vigorous-intensity aerobic physical activity throughout the week, or an equivalent combination of moderate- and vigorous-intensity activity.
2. Aerobic activity should be performed in bouts of at least ten minutes' duration.
3. For additional health benefits, adults should increase their moderate-intensity aerobic physical activity to 300 minutes per week, or engage in 150 minutes of vigorous-intensity aerobic physical activity per week, or an equivalent combination of moderate- and vigorous-intensity activity.
4. Muscle-strengthening activities should be done involving major muscle groups on two or more days a week.

Adults aged 65 and above

1. Older adults should do at least 150 minutes of moderate-intensity aerobic physical activity throughout the week, or do at least 75 minutes of vigorous-intensity aerobic physical activity throughout the week, or an equivalent combination of moderate- and vigorous-intensity activity.
2. Aerobic activity should be performed in bouts of at least ten minutes' duration.

(Continued)

Box 6.2 World Health Organization recommendations on physical activity for health (*cont.*)

3. For additional health benefits, older adults should increase their moderate-intensity aerobic physical activity to 300 minutes per week, or engage in 150 minutes of vigorous-intensity aerobic physical activity per week, or an equivalent combination of moderate- and vigorous-intensity activity.
4. Older adults with poor mobility should perform physical activity to enhance balance and prevent falls on three or more days per week.
5. Muscle-strengthening activities, involving major muscle groups, should be done on two or more days a week.
6. When older adults cannot do the recommended amounts of physical activity because of health conditions, they should be as physically active as their abilities and conditions allow.

Regular physical activity is also positively associated with aspects of psychological and social health, although evidence of causal effects is more limited. Reviews have indicated that choices to participate in enjoyable, organised team sport can be especially likely to lead to well-being benefits (Eime *et al.* 2013a). Commonly cited benefits among young people

Figure 6.2 Recommended levels of physical activity

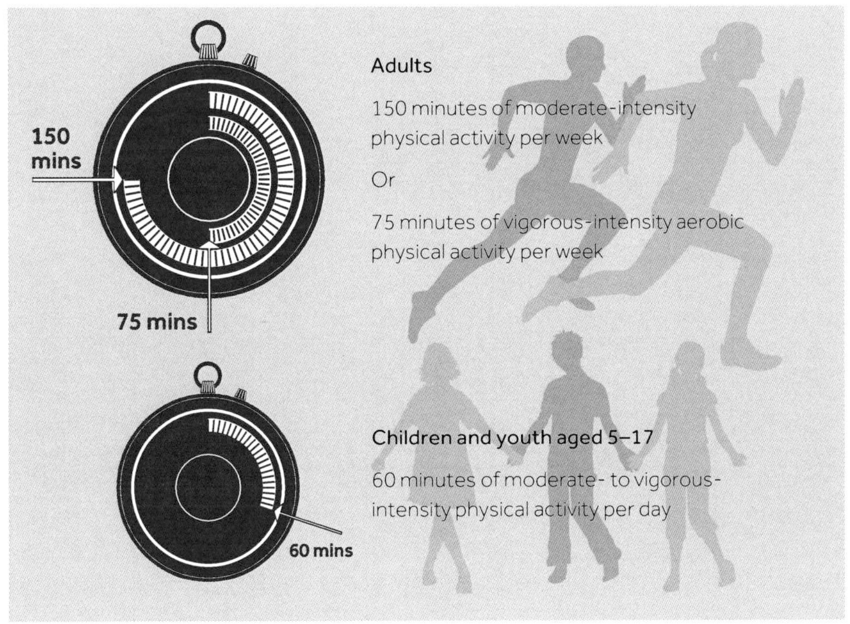

Source: WHO (2010)

include lower social anxiety, lower social isolation, better social self-concept and improved self-esteem (Eime *et al.* 2013). Psychological outcomes, including reduced stress and distress, are more commonly reported among adults (Eime *et al.* 2013). Studies also indicate the potential value of carefully designed and implemented sport-based initiatives for reducing mental health problems among adults and young people (Biddle and Asare 2011). The potential of sport-based approaches to contribute to well-being in respect of aspects of social inclusion is further considered through SDGs 4, 5 and 16.

Despite these potential benefits for physical and mental health and all aspects of well-being, WHO data from 2010 indicate the worrying scale of inactive populations: globally, 20 per cent of adult males and 27 per cent of adult women do not fulfil recommended levels of physical activity. Equivalent data for young people aged 11–17 years are especially concerning, with 78 per cent of boys and 84 per cent of girls being insufficiently active in respect of age-appropriate recommendations (WHO 2014b). Comparative levels of inactivity are lower in low- and middle-income countries, standing at 12 per cent and 24 per cent of adult males and females, respectively. However, policy impetus in such countries remains important, as comparatively higher levels of occupational, domestic and transport-related physical activity are threatened by prominent economic, social and environmental changes (Kohl *et al.* 2012; WHO 2015b).

Greater policy alignment, co-ordination and learning across different sectors, including sport, are advised to address the multi-faceted causes of physical inactivity and achieve population-level change.

In general, public health and other policy responses to physical inactivity have previously not received the same priority as other factors linked to non-communicable diseases: tobacco, alcohol and diet (Kohl *et al.* 2012). The WHO estimates that around 80 per cent of countries had policies and plans to address physical inactivity in 2013, but there is common recognition of significant weaknesses in implementation (Kohl *et al.* 2012; WHO 2015b; GoPA [n.d.]). Greater policy alignment, co-ordination and learning across different sectors, including sport, are advised to address the multi-faceted causes of physical inactivity and achieve population-level change (Heath *et al.* 2012). Addressing disparities in health outcomes also requires co-ordinated action, given that various risk factors affecting health and well-being – including access to sport and active recreation (Nicholson *et al.* 2010) – are linked to broader economic and social inequalities that cut across a number of SDGs.

Effective national policy development specifically needs to be informed by appropriate evidence. Internationally recognised survey tools are available for the collection of disaggregated data on physical activity (WHO 2008; Bull *et al.* 2009). However, across many countries, resources for continuous monitoring of population-level physical activity are limited (Hallal *et al.* 2012). In response to this need, and with the support of the WHO, the Global Physical Activity Observatory was instigated in 2016 to offer a hub for validated, country-specific physical activity statistics (Hallal *et al.* 2014). The Observatory also seeks to address the current lack of academic research that may specifically inform physical activity policies in low- and middle-income countries (Khoo and Morris 2012; Hallal *et al.* 2014).

Enhanced data and evidence can improve differentiation within policy responses. For example, interventions for people with a disability need to be based on clear understanding of the particular barriers and varying levels of participation that can be found among those with specific impairments. Differentiated policy is also required to contribute to improving physical activity across the life-course. Education policies that ensure that all children acquire fundamental movement competencies are important, given that physical inactivity and sedentary behaviours among children can track through to adulthood (Biddle *et al.* 2010). However, there should be no complacency that participation among young people will automatically translate into lifelong physical activity habits (Green 2014). There is a specific need to enable continued participation over periods of transition across the life-course (Allender *et al.* 2008), and recognition of the importance of harnessing social networks, especially among older-age adults, to encourage physical activity (King and King 2010; Shaw *et al.* 2010).

Education policies that ensure that all children acquire fundamental movement competencies are important, given that physical inactivity and sedentary behaviours among children can track through to adulthood.

Incentivising active lifestyles for communities and work places

Botswana

Ministry of Youth Empowerment, Sports and Culture Development
Government of Botswana

The health cost and impact of non-communicable disease in Botswana is steadily increasing. Non-communicable diseases are now estimated to account for thirty-seven percent of mortality in Botswana (WHO 2014c). Physical inactivity is one of the main risk factors for non-communicable disease. In Botswana, 33 per cent of women and 28 per cent of men over the age of 18 do not undertake sufficient levels of physical activity (GoPA 2014).

(Continued)

Incentivising active lifestyles for communities and work places (*cont.*)

In response, the government of Botswana, through its Ministry of Youth Empowerment, Sports and Culture, has taken a step towards promoting active lifestyles beyond just setting policy and carrying out advocacy. Acting in line with its National Sport and Recreation Policy and the Botswana National Fitness Policy, as well as with a view to contributing to SDG target 3.4 on reducing premature mortality from non-communicable disease, the government of Botswana is incentivising sport participation and physically active lifestyles.

It is doing this by devoting at least two hours of business time every last Friday of each month to workplace physical activity. Under this programme, all employees of the public sector (who represent the majority of the labour force in Botswana) are released to participate in workplace-organised sport or physical activity without any loss of income or adverse consequences. Government departments and agencies also have the flexibility to choose the day or week of the month in which they wish to dedicate time to this activity.

To implement this, suitably qualified wellness officers and volunteers are being engaged to develop suitable programmes for their workplaces.

In addition in line with national policy, the government has recently deployed officers in all ten districts that make up local government in Botswana, to mobilise private sector and community stakeholders to emulate the government in the promotion of active lifestyles and in other, youth-related, empowerment programmes. To this end, the government, through its departments and agencies, will provide, free of charge, its facilities, such as stadiums, gyms, halls and open spaces, for this and related programmes.

To complement existing policies and programmes, the government is also supporting sporting associations and schools sport organisations to develop targeted age-specific sport and physical activity frameworks as part of its Long-Term Athlete Development Strategy, which is the country's model for advancing long-term, sustainable participation in sport and physical activity, as well as sporting success.

More generally, policies that span sport, physical activity, and public and mental health should take strong account of the variety of social, cultural and environmental factors that may contribute to physical inactivity among particular groups.

More generally, policies that span sport, physical activity, and public and mental health should take strong account of the variety of social, cultural and environmental factors that may contribute to physical inactivity among particular groups (Bauman *et al.* 2012). Existing initiatives that have proved to be locally effective in adopting targeted approaches can provide valuable lessons that may be more broadly replicated. At the other end of the spectrum, and in those countries subject to rapid urbanisation, creating appropriate physical infrastructure can make a widespread contribution to engagement in physical activity (Kaczynski and Henderson 2007), with policy options to do this further considered in relation to SDG 11.

Evidence also supports the efficacy of communication and information campaigns to promote engagement in sport and physical activity that have, as yet, mainly been implemented in medium- and high-income countries (Heath *et al.* 2012). Targeting messages at particular population groups remains most effective as part of high-intensity, cross-sectoral campaigns that utilise a range of communication media (Heath *et al.* 2012). High profile sport events can provide particular opportunities for population-level communication. As recent examples indicate (Weed *et al.* 2015), event-based communication to increase awareness and motivation needs to be well-integrated into broader strategies to ensure that associated opportunities for participation are readily accessible.

Target 3.3 By 2030, end the epidemics of AIDS, tuberculosis, malaria and neglected tropical diseases, and combat hepatitis, water-borne diseases and other communicable diseases.

Target 3.5 Strengthen the prevention and treatment of substance abuse, including narcotic drug abuse and harmful use of alcohol.

Target 3.7 By 2030, ensure universal access to sexual and reproductive healthcare services, including for family planning, information and education, and the integration of reproductive health into national strategies and programmes.

Many existing sport-based initiatives seek to educate and empower participants to contribute to the prevention of a range of health problems. The global spread of such initiatives reflects the flexibility of the sport-based approaches that have been used to address different communicable diseases, sexual and reproductive health, and substance abuse. Although evidence remains inconclusive on the preventive efficacy of all sport-based approaches, a systematic review found that sport-based initiatives that sought to contribute to AIDS prevention increased specific knowledge and reported condom use, at least in the short term (Kaufman *et al.* 2013).

The particular contribution of many initiatives commonly rests on the popularity of sport among important population groups. Sport can be a way of attracting and engaging young people who may otherwise suffer from various forms of exclusion, and so may not be reached by traditional forms of health education. More generally, sport-based approaches may be particularly valuable in contexts where growing populations of young people are often at higher risk of communicable and sexually

Sport can be a way of attracting and engaging young people who may otherwise suffer from various forms of exclusion, and so may not be reached by traditional forms of health education.

transmitted diseases (WHO 2014a). Involving girls and young women and ensuring inclusion more broadly can also contribute to addressing the stigmatisation commonly associated with AIDS and other communicable diseases.

Engaging in sport in itself may act as a diversion from contexts which are associated with health-risk behaviours. However, the limitations of diversion-effects in isolation are emphasised, given that sport can be an opportunity for both alcohol and drug abuse. Sport-based approaches that also seek to enable social and community development have therefore been widely recognised as having greater potential (Mwaanga and Banda 2014), especially where they provide safe spaces in which young people can discuss health and social problems with peers and trusted coaches. Numerous curricula have now been developed to inform scaled-up training in sport-based active learning for health and other social issues (Cronin 2011). However, care must be taken by all stakeholders to ensure that the implementation of sport-based curricula is contextually relevant and does not solely individualise responsibility for health behaviour (Forde 2014).

Empowerment for disease prevention, therefore, depends on multi-layered approaches that also address contextual and structural barriers that inhibit behaviour change (Jeanes 2013). This calls for the alignment of particular sport-based initiatives with broader policies and cross-sectoral implementation. Reciprocal contributions by sport and health agencies can enhance the delivery of specific initiatives. Examples point to the valued input of health practitioners to sport-based education and, conversely, delivery by sport practitioners that supports engagement in health initiatives (Lindsey and Banda 2011). Such synergies can be further enabled, enhanced and expanded through working towards well-aligned policies across different and relevant sectors at both national and local levels.

The implementation of policy options, including those for sport-based approaches, needs to address issues of scale and enable differentiated responses where appropriate.

6.3 The means of implementation: Policy options for Sustainable Development Goal 3

SDG 3 relates to population-level health problems that, equally, can have a profound impact upon particular individuals and groups. Therefore, the implementation of policy options, including those for sport-based approaches, needs to address issues of scale and enable differentiated responses where appropriate. The need for differentiation is further emphasised, as contributions to aspects of health can be made through both participation in and through sport. Implementing at scale requires appropriate financial resources, but can also use information- and communication-based policy instruments to contribute to health education. Improved data and information is also important to inform the effective targeting of some sport-based approaches. Similarly, implementation towards capacity-building can contribute to scaled impact but also enhance specifically targeted initiatives.

Table 6.1 Policy options to enhance the contribution of sport to SDG 3

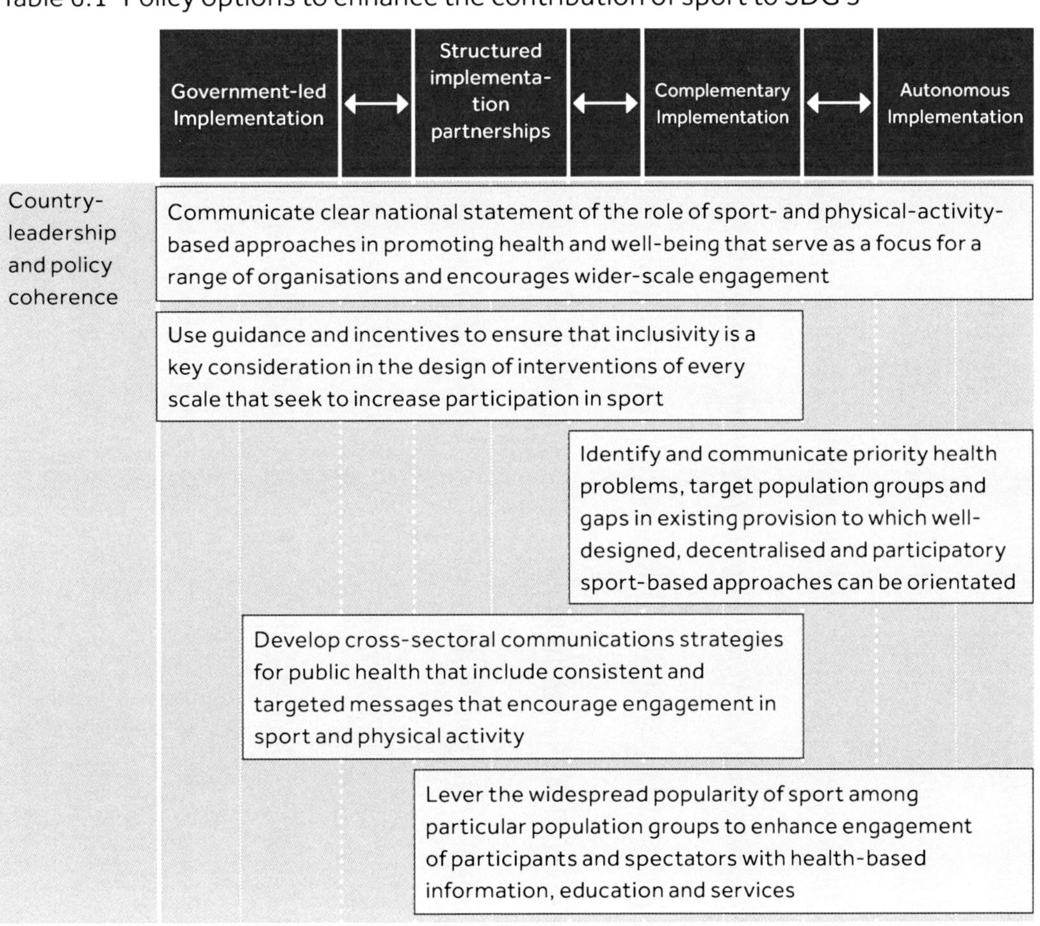

	Government-led Implementation	⟷	Structured implementa-tion partnerships	⟷	Complementary Implementation	⟷	Autonomous Implementation
Country-leadership and policy coherence	Communicate clear national statement of the role of sport- and physical-activity-based approaches in promoting health and well-being that serve as a focus for a range of organisations and encourages wider-scale engagement						
	Use guidance and incentives to ensure that inclusivity is a key consideration in the design of interventions of every scale that seek to increase participation in sport						
					Identify and communicate priority health problems, target population groups and gaps in existing provision to which well-designed, decentralised and participatory sport-based approaches can be orientated		
	Develop cross-sectoral communications strategies for public health that include consistent and targeted messages that encourage engagement in sport and physical activity						
			Lever the widespread popularity of sport among particular population groups to enhance engagement of participants and spectators with health-based information, education and services				

(Continued)

Table 6.1 Policy options to enhance the contribution of sport to SDG 3 (*cont.*)

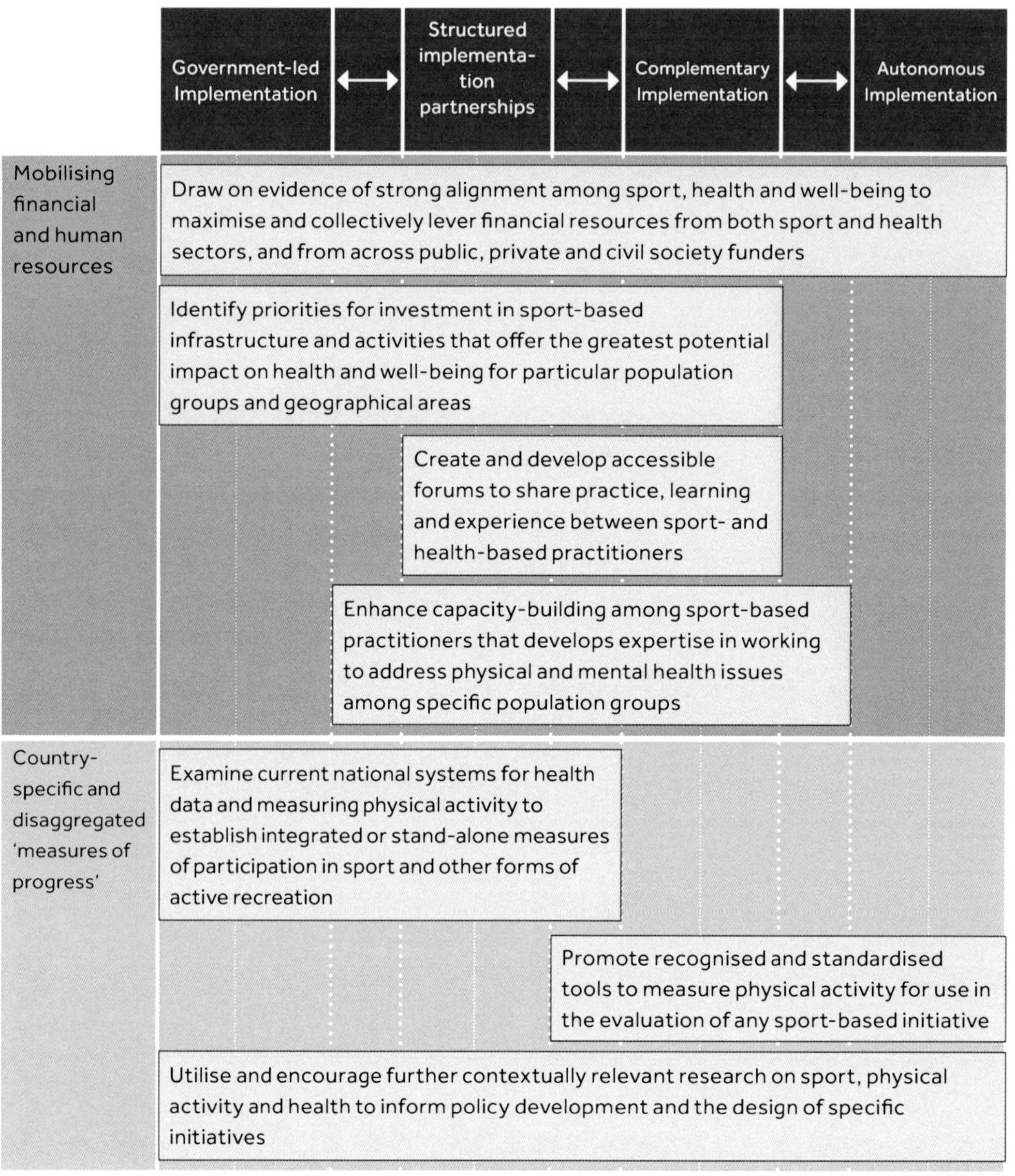

	Government-led Implementation	⟷	Structured implementation partnerships	⟷	Complementary Implementation	⟷	Autonomous Implementation
Mobilising financial and human resources	Draw on evidence of strong alignment among sport, health and well-being to maximise and collectively lever financial resources from both sport and health sectors, and from across public, private and civil society funders						
	Identify priorities for investment in sport-based infrastructure and activities that offer the greatest potential impact on health and well-being for particular population groups and geographical areas						
			Create and develop accessible forums to share practice, learning and experience between sport- and health-based practitioners				
		Enhance capacity-building among sport-based practitioners that develops expertise in working to address physical and mental health issues among specific population groups					
Country-specific and disaggregated 'measures of progress'	Examine current national systems for health data and measuring physical activity to establish integrated or stand-alone measures of participation in sport and other forms of active recreation						
				Promote recognised and standardised tools to measure physical activity for use in the evaluation of any sport-based initiative			
	Utilise and encourage further contextually relevant research on sport, physical activity and health to inform policy development and the design of specific initiatives						

References

Allender, S., L. Hutchinson and C. Foster (2008), 'Life-change events and participation in physical activity: a systematic review', *Health Promotion International*, Vol. 23, 160–172.

Bauman, A. E., R. S. Reis, J. F. Sallis, J. C. Wells, R. J. F. Loos and B. W. Martin (2012), 'Correlates of physical activity: why are some people physically active and others not?', *The Lancet*, Vol. 380, 258–271.

Biddle, S. J., N. Pearson, G. M. Ross and R. Braithwaite (2010), 'Tracking of sedentary behaviours of young people: a systematic review', *Preventive Medicine*, Vol. 51, 345–351.

Biddle, S. J. and M. Asare (2011), 'Physical activity and mental health in children and adolescents: a review of reviews', *British Journal of Sports Medicine*, Vol. 45, 886–895.

Bull, F. C., T. S. Maslin and T. Armstrong (2009), 'Global physical activity questionnaire (GPAQ): nine country reliability and validity study', *Journal of Physical Activity and Health*, Vol. 6, 790–804.

Commonwealth Secretariat (2015), *Commonwealth Health Ministers Meeting 2015: Ministerial Statement*, May 2015, available at: http://thecommonwealth.org/media/news/commonwealth-health-ministers-meeting-2015-ministerial-statement

Cronin, Ó. (2011), *Comic Relief Review: Mapping the Research on the Impact of Sport and Development Interventions*, Orla Cronin Research, Manchester, available at: http://www.sportanddev.org/en/connect/userprofile.cfm?3096/Comic-Relief-Research-Mapping

Davis, J. C., E. Verhagen, S. Bryan, T. Liu-Ambrose, J. Borland, D. Buchner, M. R. C. Hendriks, R. Weiler, J. R. Morrow Jr, W. van Mechelen, S. N. Blair, M. Pratt, J. Windt, H. al-Tunaiji, E. Macri and K. M. Khan (2014), '2014 Consensus statement from the first Economics of Physical Inactivity Consensus (EPIC) conference (Vancouver)', *British Journal of Sports Medicine*, Vol. 48, 947–951.

Eime, R. M., J. A. Young, J. T. Harvey, M. J. Charity and W. R. Payne (2013), 'A systematic review of the psychological and social benefits of participation in sport for adults: informing development of a conceptual model of health through sport', *International Journal of Behavioral Nutrition and Physical Activity*, Vol. 10, 98.

Forde, S. D. (2014), 'Look after yourself, or look after one another? An analysis of life skills in Sport for Development and Peace HIV prevention curriculum', *Sociology of Sport Journal*, Vol. 31, 287–303.

Global Observatory for Physical Activity (GoPA) (n.d.), *Facts*, available at: http://www.globalphysicalactivityobservatory.com/facts/

Global Observatory for Physical Activity (GoPA) (2014) *Physical activity Country Card*, available at: http://www.globalphysicalactivityobservatory.com/card/?country=BW

Green, K. (2014), 'Mission impossible? Reflecting upon the relationship between physical education, youth sport and lifelong participation', *Sport, Education and Society*, Vol. 19, 357–375.

Hallal, P. C., L. B. Andersen, F. C. Bull, R. Guthold, W. Haskell and U. Ekelund (2012), 'Global physical activity levels: surveillance progress, pitfalls, and prospects', *The Lancet*, Vol. 380, 247–257.

Hallal, P. C., R. C. Martins and A. Ramírez (2014), 'The Lancet Physical Activity Observatory: promoting physical activity worldwide', *The Lancet*, Vol. 384, 471–472.

Heath, G. W., D. C. Parra, O. L. Sarmiento, MD, L. B. Andersen, N. Owen, S. Goenka, F. Montes and R. C. Brownson (2012), 'Evidence-based intervention in physical activity: lessons from around the world', *The Lancet*, Vol. 380, 272–281.

Jeanes, R. (2013), 'Educating through sport? Examining HIV/AIDS education and sport-for-development through the perspectives of Zambian young people', *Sport, Education and Society*, Vol. 18, 388–406.

Kaczynski, A. T. and K. A. Henderson (2007), 'Environmental correlates of physical activity: a review of evidence about parks and recreation', *Leisure Sciences*, Vol. 29, 315–354.

Kaufman, Z. A., T. S. Spencer and D. A. Ross (2013), 'Effectiveness of sport-based HIV prevention interventions: a systematic review of the evidence', *AIDS and Behavior*, Vol. 17, 987–1001.

Khoo, S. and T. Morris (2012), 'Physical activity and obesity research in the Asia-Pacific: A review', *Asia-Pacific Journal of Public Health*, Vol. 24, 435–449.

King, A. C. and D. K. King (2010), 'Physical activity for an aging population', *Public Health Review*, Vol. 32, 401–426.

Kohl, H. W., C. L. Craig, E. V. Lambert, S. Inoue, J. R. Alkandari, G. Leetongin and S. Kahlmeier (2012), 'The pandemic of physical inactivity: global action for public health', *The Lancet*, Vol. 380 (9838), 294–305.

Lindsey, I. and D. Banda (2011), 'Sport and the fight against HIV/AIDS in Zambia: A "partnership" approach?', *International Review of Sociology of Sport*, Vol. 46, 90–107.

Mwaanga, O. and D. Banda (2014), 'A postcolonial approach to understanding sport-based empowerment of people living with HIV/AIDS (PLWHA) in Zambia: The case of the cultural philosophy of Ubuntu', *Journal of Disability and Religion*, Vol. 18, 173–191.

Nicholson, M., R. Hoye and B. Houlihan (Eds) (2010), *Participation in Sport: International Policy Perspectives*, Routledge, Abingdon.

Shaw, B. A., J. Liang, N. Krause, M. Gallant and K. McGeever (2010), 'Age differences and social stratification in the long-term trajectories of leisure-time physical activity', *The Journals of Gerontology Series B: Psychological Sciences and Social Sciences*, Vol. 65, 756–766.

Weed, M., E. Coren, J. Fiore, I. Wellard, D. Chatziefstathiou, L. Mansfield and S. Dowse (2015), 'The Olympic Games and raising sport participation: a systematic review of evidence and an interrogation of policy for a demonstration effect', *European Sport Management Quarterly*, Vol. 15, 195–226.

World Health Organization (WHO) (2008), *A framework to monitor and evaluate the implementation of the Global Strategy on Diet, Physical Activity and Health*, available at: http://www.who.int/dietphysicalactivity/DPASindicators/en/

World Health Organization (WHO) (2010), *Global Recommendations on Physical Activity for Health*, available at: http://whqlibdoc.who.int/publications/2010/9789241599979_eng.pdf

World Health Organization (WHO) (2014a), *Adolescents: Health Risks and Solutions Fact Sheet*, available at: http://www.who.int/mediacentre/factsheets/fs345/en/

World Health Organization (WHO) (2014b), *Global Status Report on Non-communicable Diseases 2014*, available at: http://www.who.int/nmh/publications/ncd-status-report-2014/en/

World Health Organization (WHO) (2014c), *Non-communicable Diseases (NCD) Country Profiles, 2014*, available at: http://www.who.int/nmh/countries/bwa_en.pdf

World Health Organization (WHO) (2015a), *Non-communicable Diseases Fact Sheet*, available at: http://www.who.int/mediacentre/factsheets/fs355/en/

World Health Organization (WHO) (2015b), *Physical Activity Fact Sheet*, available at: http://www.who.int/mediacentre/factsheets/fs385/en/

Chapter 7
Ensure Inclusive and Equitable Quality Education and Promote Lifelong Learning Opportunities for All (SDG 4)

7.1 Introduction

The *2030 Agenda for Sustainable Development* offers a transformative and universal vision that commits to the provision of inclusive and equitable quality education at all levels, for all people and across the life-course. The scope of this holistic vision builds on the advances made across the period of the MDGs, during which net enrolment rates in primary education increased from 83 to 91 per cent in developing regions of the world (United Nations 2015). As reinforced by the *Incheon Declaration* of the 2015 World Education Forum (World Education Forum 2015), education and lifelong learning are recognised through SDG 4 as being fundamental human rights and as vital in realising the broader aspirations of the *2030 Agenda for Sustainable Development*.

Provision for physical education and sport-based activities within schools and other formal and informal education settings can make various contributions to SDG 4 and its targets. High-quality physical education is essential to young people's development of physical literacy and can enhance wider educational outcomes in line with SDG target 4.1 (see Box 7.1). The focus of SDG target 4.5 on inclusion and equality highlights the need to make physical education and sport-based activities accessible by all, and also the need to enhance the potential contribution that such activities can make to engage particular groups in both formal and informal education. Finally, many sport-based initiatives have also been oriented towards the holistic development and empowerment of young people and the dissemination of educational messages, and so are relevant to SDG targets 4.4 and 4.7.

Provision for physical education and sport-based activities within schools and other formal and informal education settings can make various contributions to SDG 4 and its targets.

Box 7.1 Enhancing the contribution of sport to Sustainable Development Goal 4: Key policy implications

- Physical education and sport-based activities in schools play an essential role in developing the skills and competencies required for long-term engagement in physical activity, and its concomitant health and well-being benefits.
- There is also good evidence regarding the contribution that high-quality physical education and sport-based activity can make across a range of other educational outcomes.
- Sport-based activities may be attractive to some who may be otherwise disengaged from educational provision, but, equally, teachers and others delivering physical education need to ensure that provision is inclusive of all young people.
- Capacity-building and training for those delivering physical education and sport-based activities is a priority, in order to ensure high-quality and inclusive practice.
- Policy impetus is commonly required to ensure the implementation of existing commitments to physical education together with increasing its status within education systems.

7.2 Analysis of sport and specific SDG targets

Target 4.1 By 2030, ensure that all girls and boys complete free, equitable and quality primary and secondary education leading to relevant and effective learning outcomes.

Multiple international conventions and declarations have recognised the importance of physical education, physical activity and sport as a fundamental right for all.

Multiple international conventions and declarations have recognised the importance of physical education, physical activity and sport as a fundamental right for all (United Nations 1989; UNESCO 2013a; UNESCO 2015a) Aligned specifically with SDG 4.1, the revised *International Charter of Physical Education, Physical Activity and Sport* that was adopted in 2015 by all UNESCO member states declares that:

> *Each education system must assign the requisite place and importance to physical education, physical activity and sport in order to establish a balance and strengthen links between physical activities and other components of education.*
>
> (UNESCO 2015a, 3)

As a constituent part of holistic education, formative childhood experiences are essential to the development of physical literacy. Older children and adults who have not gained fundamental movement proficiencies – or the knowledge, confidence and motivation that also contribute to physical literacy – face significant and lifelong barriers to involvement in physical activity and sport (Whitehead 2010; Giblin *et al.* 2014). Conversely, those children who do gain the foundations of movement patterns from an early age are well placed to develop more fine-grained skills through late childhood and into adulthood. Evidence indicates that young people do not develop physical literacy and its underpinning range of movement skills and proficiencies automatically (Fairclough *et al.* 2002; Bailey *et al.* 2009). It follows that Physical education, complemented by other sporting opportunities, is vital to the development of movement competencies and all other aspects of physical literacy among young people. As recognised in UNESCO's policy guidance for *Quality Physical Education* (UNESCO 2015b), all children must, therefore, have regular and sufficient access to age-appropriate opportunities for physical education and sport-based activity as a fundamental component of education, and to enable and enhance lifelong physical activity, with its benefits for all aspects of health and well-being (SDG 5).

Physical education, complemented by other sporting opportunities, is vital to the development of movement competencies and all other aspects of physical literacy among young people.

A range of further contributions to young people's personal, social and educational development can also be made through high-quality opportunities for physical education and sport-based activity. Reviews of research (Coalter 2007; Bailey *et al.* 2009) indicate that:

- enjoyable experiences of physical education and sport-based activity, which enable young people to feel a sense of competence and skill mastery, can contribute to improvements in self-esteem and self-confidence
- skilled leaders can use multiple 'teachable moments' during and after activities to promote and reinforce values such as fair play, teamwork and respect for rules and other people
- movement activities and games can be utilised and adapted to contribute to knowledge acquisition relevant to other academic subjects
- relationships between young people and teachers can be improved within and through physical education and sport, especially as non-classroom settings provide opportunities for the adoption of non-traditional and child-centred pedagogical approaches

- students' concentration, arousal and broader engagement in school may be enhanced through appropriately managed and timed activities.

It should be stressed that these benefits may not be automatically derived from participation in physical education and sport-based activity. Further claims of overall effects on educational attainment also require careful, context-specific and methodologically rigorous evaluation (Coalter 2007).

While physical education has been declared compulsory in 97 per cent of countries, levels and quality of provision often vary significantly across countries, localities and schools.

Nevertheless, the development of education policy in respect of physical education and sport-based activity in school settings can be valuably informed by considering the contextual relevance of various overarching concerns. While physical education has been declared compulsory in 97 per cent of countries, levels and quality of provision often vary significantly across countries, localities and schools (UNESCO 2013b). In 29 per cent of countries, physical education is not implemented in accordance with mandatory obligations or policy guidance (UNESCO 2013b). Enhancing implementation of statutory requirements requires specific and ongoing reinforcement of the status of physical education, especially given general pressures on educational systems and customary prioritisation of other subjects (UNESCO 2013b). Education-wide systems of monitoring and quality assurance, which can be informed by UNESCO's benchmarks for quality physical education (UNESCO 2015b), can provide incentives for compliance and enable identification of specific areas for improvement.

High-quality provision is essential to enable the realisation of all educational benefits of physical education and sport.

High-quality provision is essential to enable the realisation of all educational benefits of physical education and sport. The differentiation of activities can support universal engagement, especially as some young people are less likely to engage if competition is inappropriately promoted (Fairclough *et al.* 2002; Wilkinson *et al.* 2013). In particular contexts, indigenous games can also be valuably implemented as part of educational curricula (Burnett 2009; Chepyator-Thomson 2014). Such requirements for high-quality provision point to the importance of widespread, but effectively differentiated, training for teachers and others who contribute to physical education and sport in school settings (Morgan and Hansen 2008; Wang and Ha 2009).

In a number of contexts, enhancing the capacity and confidence of primary school teachers to deliver physical education is a priority (UNESCO 2013b; Keim and de Coning 2014; Sanders *et al.* 2014). Ensuring sport coaches are appropriately qualified and conversant with their role in fostering the wider personal and educational development of young people can be a priority where their contribution to provision in schools is increasing (Cope *et al.* 2015). Skilled staff can deliver physical education and sport in a variety of conditions. However, as further considered in relation to SDG 11, working towards ensuring access to appropriate facilities and equipment – especially in the 57 per cent of countries where these are regarded as limited or insufficient – can make important contributions to young people's engagement and learning in physical education and sport (UNESCO 2013b).

Target 4.5 By 2030, eliminate gender disparities in education and ensure equal access to all levels of education and vocational training for the vulnerable, including persons with disabilities, indigenous peoples and children in vulnerable situations.

Addressing disparities of access to physical education and sport-based activity in education settings is important in itself, and can also make further, long-term contributions to the development of more inclusive societies. Ensuring that inequalities are eliminated in school contexts from early ages is vital for sustained inclusion in physical activity and sport. Participation by young people who may otherwise face exclusion – for example, girls and people with disabilities – can raise awareness and address wider discriminatory misconceptions across communities and societies (UNICEF 2013). However, progress towards inclusion in physical education is variable across localities and vulnerable groups. While there have been some positive trends towards equal access and provision for girls, there has been little global change in access to physical education for people with disabilities (UNESCO 2013b).

While policy development needs to take account of the local contexts and different barriers that affect groups suffering from exclusion, some important principles for working towards equal access to physical education can be identified. Mainstreaming and child-centred pedagogies are central to reducing existing inequalities (UNESCO 2015b). Implementing flexible and inclusive curricula requires well-trained teachers with appropriate knowledge, skills and awareness (Vickerman 2007). The provision of specialist teachers and addressing inadequate facilities and equipment is especially important where, in particular, people with disabilities may suffer exclusion from physical education. Wider efforts to address societal barriers to inclusion are also an important component of strategies to promote inclusion in physical education (UNESCO 2015b).

Play for the Advancement of Quality Education

Ghana, Mozambique, Pakistan, Rwanda and Tanzania

Heather Barnabe
Senior Manager
Global Programme Partnerships
Right To Play International

Andrea Diaz-Varela
Education Specialist
Global Program Development
Right To Play International

Right To Play has used sport and play since 2001 to educate and empower children and young people across 20 countries. Currently the organisation is harnessing the power of play to improve education outcomes with the implementation of Play for the Advancement of Quality Education (PAQE) in five commonwealth countries: Ghana, Mozambique, Pakistan, Rwanda and Tanzania. PAQE aims to influence the policy and regulatory environment in these countries to support the integration of play-based learning to enhance quality education. While the benefits of play as an active learning, pedagogical tool to improve learning outcomes have been recognised, many countries lack the implementation of policies and a supportive regulatory environment.

The Government of Rwanda has been determined to bridge the gap between policy and implementation. The Ministry of Education (MINEDUC) through the Rwanda Education Board (REB) initiated a revision of the national pre-primary, primary and secondary curriculum in July 2013. This aimed to shift the curriculum from a knowledge- to a competence-based curriculum.

Right To Play had previously provided support to REB on the development of the Physical Education and Sport Teacher Guide. In light of this successful partnership, REB asked Right To Play to join the Physical Education and Sport and the Cross-Cutting Issues panels of the curriculum review process, both sitting within the larger Curriculum Working Group. To support these efforts, Right To Play worked with stakeholders to demonstrate the effectiveness of a play-based learning methodology to deliver a curriculum on cross-cutting issues as well as physical education and sport.

REB's curriculum developers quickly recognised the potential of play-based learning approaches in delivering the competence-based curriculum across all subject areas. REB and the United Nations International Children's Emergency Fund (UNICEF), the co-chairs of the Curriculum Working Group, invited Right To Play to feed into the curriculum review for all subjects and to map play-based activities from its repository onto the 'key learnings' (competencies) of the new competence-based curriculum, across all subject areas. To support this, REB worked with teacher trainers, teachers and Right To Play staff to identify activities for specific subject topics, sub-topics and learning objectives. Participants adapted activities to target the development of specific key learnings (knowledge, attitudes and skills) under the new curriculum and integrated a

Play for the Advancement of Quality Education (*cont.*)

play-based reflect-connect-apply teaching and learning strategy into sample lesson plans.[1]

The Rwandan Ministry of Education Teacher Training Manual, which aligns with the new curriculum, identifies play-based learning as an important and beneficial active learning technique. It includes detailed background on the benefits of play and instructions on the play-based learning methodology. It also features a section on effective questioning drawing on the reflect-connect-apply teaching and learning strategy (MINEDUC 2015).

Right To Play is now working with the University of Rwanda's College of Education and REB to integrate play-based learning into the pre-service teacher training curriculum, as well as to develop sample lesson plans and the Teacher Play-Based Learning Guidelines to support implementation in the classroom.

The integration of sport and play-based learning methodology into the national curriculum, teaching resources and pre-service teacher training has the potential to contribute to SDG target 4.1, through enhancing the quality of the education environment, and to SDG target 4.5 as the methodology promotes a more inclusive learning environment and privileges different learning styles and approaches.

Rwanda's case prominently demonstrates the potential for governments to engage with international organisations and partners to support innovative approaches to sustaining education outcomes using sport and play-based approaches.

The PAQE initiative is supported by the Government of Canada through Global Affairs Canada.

1 Right To Play's RCA methodology is based on the work of educationalists such as Freire, Brown, Piaget, Brantford and others who support the concept of an educational process that is active, relevant, reflective, collaborative and applied. With its roots in experiential learning theory (Kolb 1984), RCA is a teaching strategy that guides learners through a three-step processing of their experience during a play-based learning session.

For some vulnerable or disengaged young people, targeted initiatives can draw on the popularity of sport and other forms of physical activity to facilitate their engagement with formal and non-formal education (see Figure 7.1). Individual evaluations have indicated that improved sport and physical education provision has positively contributed towards addressing problems of non-attendance in specific schools (Stead and Nevill 2010; Burnett 2014). Taking account of the particular characteristics of intended beneficiaries is a feature of well-designed initiatives. In particular, for those who may be vulnerable, the activity context must be perceived as safe and, for some, reintegration into formal education may initially be encouraged through participation in alternative environments (Sandford *et al.* 2006). A positive and supportive relationship between participants and activity leaders is recognised as a key factor in improving engagement,

For some vulnerable or disengaged young people, targeted initiatives can draw on the popularity of sport and other forms of physical activity to facilitate their engagement with formal and non-formal education.

Figure 7.1 Enhancing the contribution of sport to formal and non-formal education

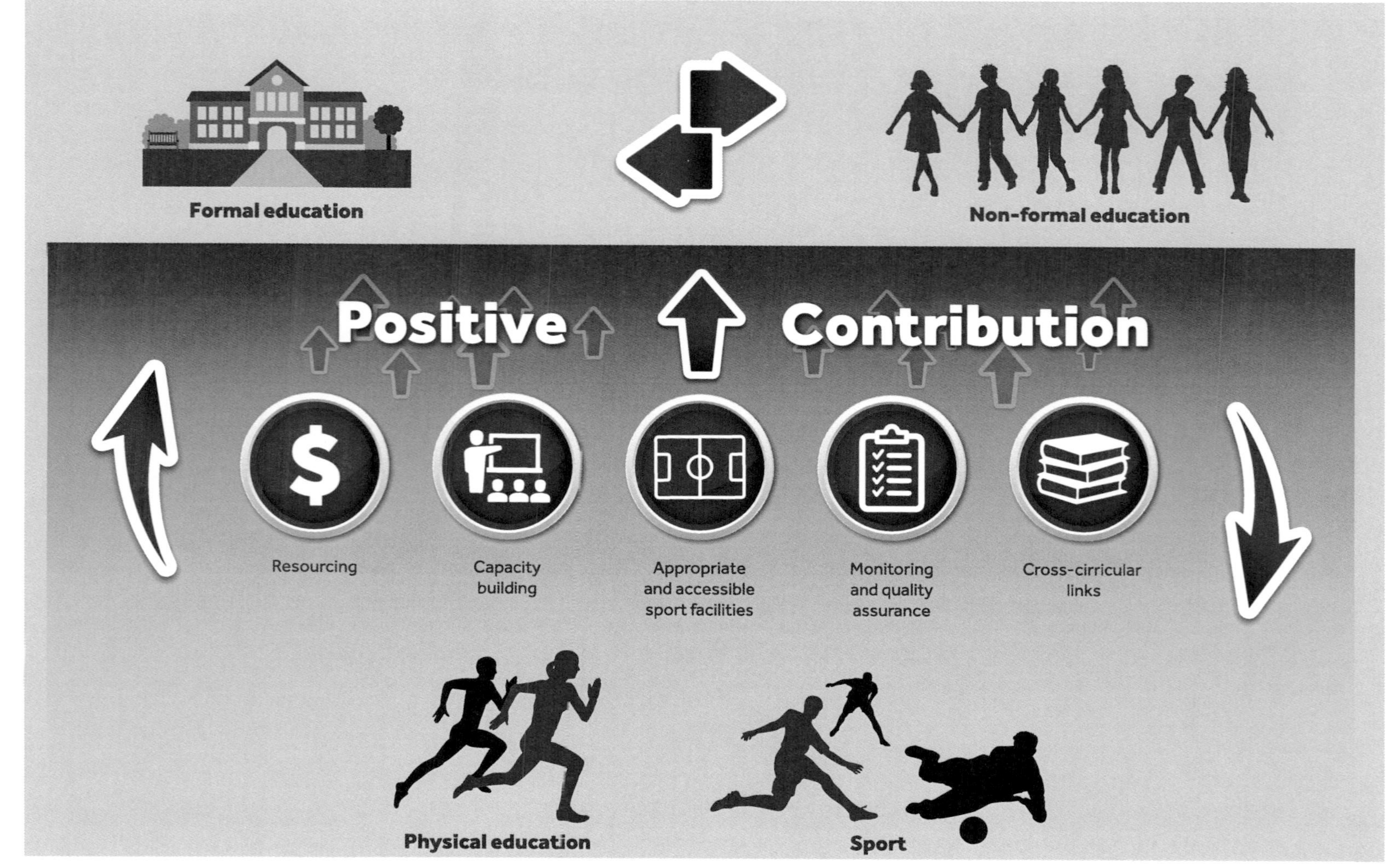

and activities that are peer led may be particularly attractive and contribute to valuable mentoring for some young people (Coalter 2013a; Nicholls 2009).

Target 4.7 By 2030, ensure that all learners acquire the knowledge and skills needed to promote sustainable development, including, among others, through education for sustainable development and sustainable lifestyles, human rights, gender equality, promotion of a culture of peace and non-violence, global citizenship, and appreciation of cultural diversity and of culture's contribution to sustainable development.

Target 4.4 By 2030, substantially increase the number of youth and adults who have relevant skills, including technical and vocational skills, for employment, decent jobs and entrepreneurship.

Numerous possibilities exist for the utilisation of sport as a forum for knowledge dissemination and for the development of skills relevant to various aspects of sustainable development. Broadly, these possibilities build on the capacity of sport to effectively and efficiently engage both young people and adults, often in large numbers and across different population groups. Perceptions of sport as a primarily leisure-based activity can both enable and inhibit its contribution as such a forum. On the one hand, the sporting environment can, in some local contexts, be seen as relatively depoliticised and free of particular cultural constraints, making it highly suitable for community integration and dissemination of potentially sensitive information (Spaaij and Schulenkorf 2014). On the other hand, sport can sometimes be dismissed or overlooked, where the significance of other development issues takes precedence (Lindsey and Banda 2011). Realising the full potential of sport requires a balanced approach that draws on the strengths of its distinctive status while complementing approaches in other sustainable development sectors.

Numerous possibilities exist for the utilisation of sport as a forum for knowledge dissemination and for the development of skills relevant to various aspects of sustainable development.

Especially when they have a high profile, sports competitions and events offer particular opportunities for broad-scale information dissemination among both participants and spectators. Marketing expertise both within and beyond sport can be harnessed to ensure that messages are effectively presented and carefully tailored towards particular audiences. New forms of social media also offer the potential for widespread engagement (GMSA 2012), although ensuring that information is distributed in forms that are locally appropriate to those engaged with sport remains vital. Furthermore, planning to use high-profile sport as a communication platform should take into consideration any risks of becoming associated with critical incidents where the integrity of sport may be compromised (see SDG 16).

Sport can also be used locally as an environment in which specifically designed experiential learning activities can contribute to youth empowerment and the acquisition of a range of 'life skills'. Young people have been supported to take peer education and leadership roles in many such interventions (Nicholls 2009; Coalter 2013b). With locally appropriate curricula and training, peer leadership can foster dialogical and mutually supportive learning and enable young people to play important roles in decentralised decision making (Wallhead and O'Sullivan 2007; Lindsey *et al.* 2016). However, systems of quality control are necessary to guard against risks that peer education could perpetuate misinformation or transgressive behaviour. Ensuring that those young people involved in peer leadership also have opportunities for progression within initiatives – and, especially, pathways whereby they can productively utilise transferable skills – is a vital consideration that is further addressed in relation to SDG 8.

7.3 The means of implementation: Policy options for Sustainable Development Goal 4

Approaches to implementation can build on the complementary alignment and mutual contributions that physical education and sport-based activities can make across formal and non-formal education.

Approaches to implementation can build on the complementary alignment and mutual contributions that physical education and sport-based activities can make across formal and non-formal education. Governments and non-state providers of education have a responsibility to ensure that physical education is appropriately resourced in all schools. Capacity-building is a key issue for all stakeholders associated with SDG 4, and consideration can usefully be given to the use of different policy instruments to encourage co-operative and complementary approaches to training for teachers, sports coaches and others involved in delivering sport-based activities in formal and informal educational settings. Even if sport-based initiatives operate autonomously or semi-autonomously, information sharing with educational stakeholders can also bring value to work with individual and targeted groups of young people. Finally, it can be through a combination of policy developments, and their demonstrated effectiveness, that problems associated with the relatively low status of physical education and sport within many education systems can be addressed.

Table 7.1 Policy options to enhance the contribution of sport to SDG 4

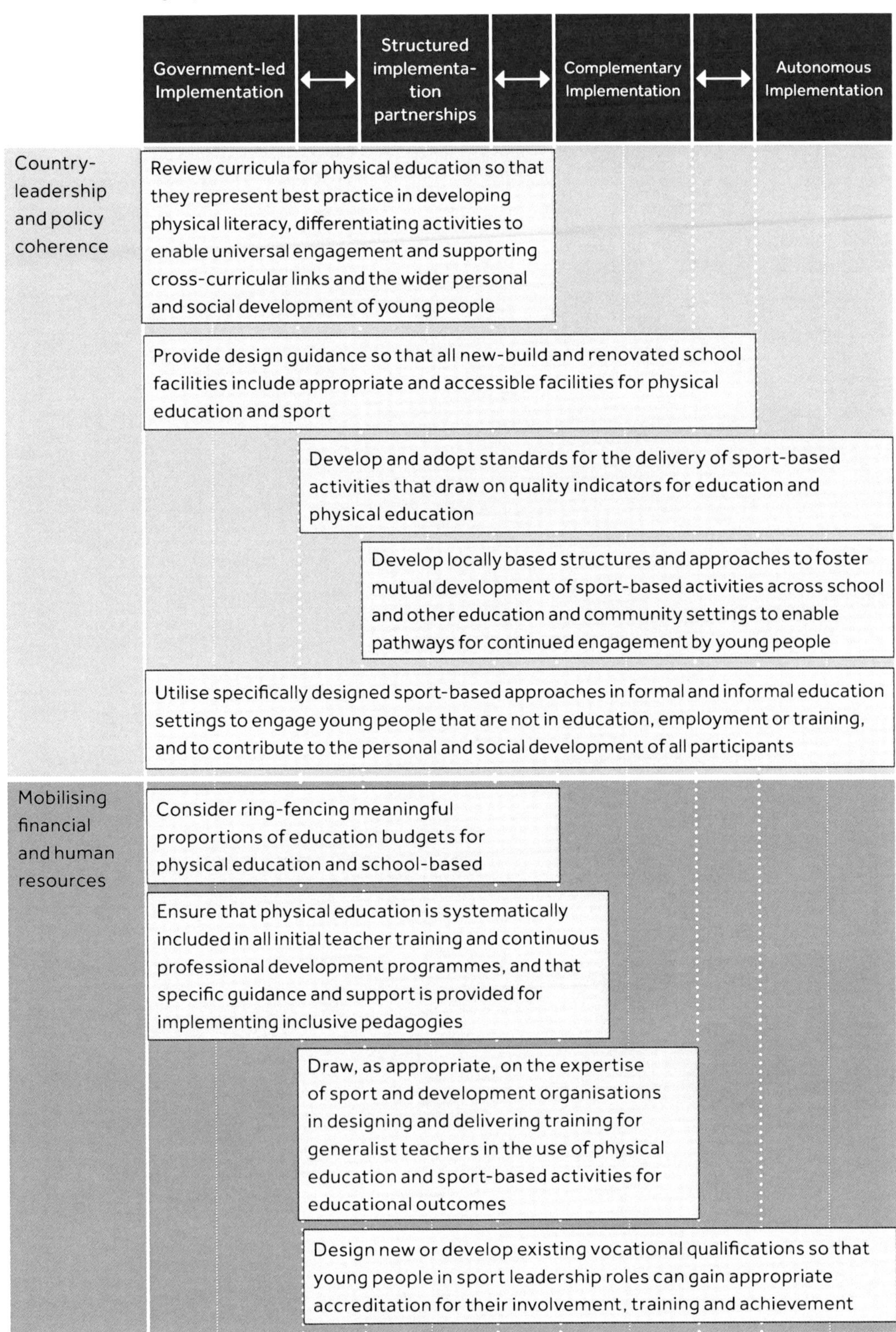

	Government-led Implementation	Structured implementation partnerships	Complementary Implementation	Autonomous Implementation
Country-leadership and policy coherence	Review curricula for physical education so that they represent best practice in developing physical literacy, differentiating activities to enable universal engagement and supporting cross-curricular links and the wider personal and social development of young people			
	Provide design guidance so that all new-build and renovated school facilities include appropriate and accessible facilities for physical education and sport			
		Develop and adopt standards for the delivery of sport-based activities that draw on quality indicators for education and physical education		
		Develop locally based structures and approaches to foster mutual development of sport-based activities across school and other education and community settings to enable pathways for continued engagement by young people		
	Utilise specifically designed sport-based approaches in formal and informal education settings to engage young people that are not in education, employment or training, and to contribute to the personal and social development of all participants			
Mobilising financial and human resources	Consider ring-fencing meaningful proportions of education budgets for physical education and school-based			
	Ensure that physical education is systematically included in all initial teacher training and continuous professional development programmes, and that specific guidance and support is provided for implementing inclusive pedagogies			
		Draw, as appropriate, on the expertise of sport and development organisations in designing and delivering training for generalist teachers in the use of physical education and sport-based activities for educational outcomes		
		Design new or develop existing vocational qualifications so that young people in sport leadership roles can gain appropriate accreditation for their involvement, training and achievement		

(Continued)

Table 7.1 Policy options to enhance the contribution of sport to SDG 4 (*cont.*)

	Government-led Implementation	⟷	Structured implementation partnerships	⟷	Complementary Implementation	⟷	Autonomous Implementation
Country-specific and disaggregated 'measures of progress'	Ensure that measures of the provision and quality of physical education delivery are included in national systems for monitoring, reporting and accountability across all schools						
					Work at different levels towards common and integrated approaches to evaluation to triangulate evidence regarding the progress of vulnerable or disengaged individuals or groups through sport-based, non-formal and formal education activities		

References

Bailey, R., K. Armour, D. Kirk, M. Jess, I. Pickup and R. Sandford (2009), 'The educational benefits claimed for physical education and school sport: an academic review', *Research Papers in Education*, Vol. 24, 1–27.

Burnett, C. (2009), 'Engaging sport-for-development for social impact in the South African context', *Sport in Society*, Vol. 12, 1192–1205.

Burnett, C. (2014), 'The impact of a sport-for education programme in the South African context of poverty', *Sport in Society*, Vol. 17, 722–735.

Chepyator-Thomson, J. R. (2014), 'Public policy, physical education and sport in English-speaking Africa', *Physical Education and Sport Pedagogy*, Vol. 19, 512–521.

Coalter, F. (2007), *A Wider Social Role for Sport: Who's Keeping the Score?* Routledge, Abingdon.

Coalter, F. (2013a), '"There is loads of relationships here": developing a programme theory for sport-for-change programmes', *International Review for the Sociology of Sport*, Vol. 48, 594–612.

Coalter, F. (2013b), *Sport for Development: What Game are We Playing?* Routledge, Abingdon.

Cope, E., R. Bailey and D. Parnell (2015), 'Outsourcing physical education: A critical discussion', *International Journal of Physical Education*, Vol. 52, 2–11.

Fairclough, S., G. Stratton and G. Baldwin (2002), 'The contribution of secondary school physical education to lifetime physical activity', *European Physical Education Review*, Vol. 8, 69–84.

Giblin, S., D. Collins, A. MacNamara and J. Kiely (2014), '"Deliberate Preparation" as an evidence-based focus for primary physical education', *Quest*, Vol. 66, 385–395.

GMSA (2012), *Shaping the Future: Realising the Potential of Informal Learning through Mobile*, available at: http://www.gsma.com/mobilefordevelopment/wp-content/uploads/2012/05/mLearning_Report_230512_V2.pdf

Keim, M. and C. de Coning (Eds) (2014), *Sport and Development Policy in Africa: Results of a Collaborative Study of Selected Country Cases*, SUN Press, Stellenbosch.

Kolb, D. A. (1984). *Experiential Learning: Experience as the Source of Learning and Development*, Prentice-Hall, New Jersey.

Lindsey, I., T. Kay, R. Jeanes and D. Banda (2016), *Localizing Global Sport for Development*, Manchester University Press, Manchester.

Lindsey, I. and D. Banda (2011), Sport and the fight against HIV/AIDS in Zambia: A "partnership" approach?', *International Review of Sociology of Sport*, Vol. 46, 90–107.

Morgan, P. J. and V. Hansen (2008), 'Classroom teachers' perceptions of the impact of barriers to teaching physical education on the quality of physical education programs', *Research Quarterly for Exercise and Sport*, Vol. 79, 506–516.

Nicholls, S. (2009), 'On the Backs of Peer Educators: using Theory to Interrogate the Role of Young People in the Field of Sport-for-Development', in Levermore, R. and A. Beacom (Eds), *Sport and International Development*, Macmillan, Basingtoke, 156–175.

Rwanda Ministry of Education (MINEDUC) (2015), *Teacher Training Manual*, Rwanda Education Board, July, 34–41.

Sanders, B., J. Phillips and B. Vanreusel (2014), 'Opportunities and challenges facing NGOs using sport as a vehicle for development in post-apartheid South Africa', *Sport, Education and Society*, Vol. 19, 789–805.

Sandford, R. A., K. M. Armour and P. C. Warmington (2006), 'Re-engaging disaffected youth through physical activity programmes', *British Educational Research Journal*, Vol. 32, 251–271.

Spaaij, R. and N. Schulenkorf (2014), 'Cultivating safe space: lessons for sport-for-development projects and events'. *Journal of Sport Management*, Vol. 28, 633–645.

Stead, R. and M. Nevill (2010), *The Impact of Physical Education and Sport on Education Outcomes: A Review of Literature*, Institute of Youth Sport, Loughborough.

UNESCO (2013a), *Declaration of Berlin*, available at: http://unesdoc.unesco.org/images/0022/002211/221114e.pdf

UNESCO (2013b), *World-wide Survey of School Physical Education*, UNESCO, Paris, 19, available at: http://unesdoc.unesco.org/images/0022/002293/229335e.pdf

UNESCO (2015a), *International Charter of Physical Education, Physical Activity and Sport*, available at: unesdoc.unesco.org/images/0023/002354/235409e.pdf

UNESCO (2015b), *Quality Physical Education: Guidelines for Policy-Makers*, available at: http://unesdoc.unesco.org/images/0023/002311/231101E.pdf

UNICEF (2013), *Sustainable Development Starts and Ends with Safe, Healthy and Well-educated Children*, available at: http://www.unicef.org/socialpolicy/files/Sustainable_Development_post_2015.pdf

United Nations (1989), *The United Nations Convention on the Rights of the Child*, available at: http://www.unicef.org.uk/Documents/Publication-pdfs/UNCRC_PRESS200910web.pdf

United Nations (2015), *The Millennium Development Goals Report 2015*, available at: http://www.un.org/millenniumgoals/2015_MDG_Report/pdf/MDG%202015%20rev%20(July%201).pdf

Vickerman, P. (2007), 'Training physical education teachers to include children with special educational needs: Perspectives from physical education initial teacher training providers', *European Physical Education Review*, Vol. 13, 385–402.

Wallhead, T. and M. O'Sullivan (2007), 'A didactic analysis of content development during the peer teaching tasks of a sport education season', *Physical Education and Sport Pedagogy*, Vol. 12, 225–243.

Wang, C. L. J. and A. S. C. Ha (2009), 'Teacher development in physical education: A review of the literature', *Asian Social Science*, Vol. 4, 3–17.

Whitehead, M. (Ed.). (2010), *Physical Literacy: Throughout the Lifecourse*, Routledge, Abingdon.

Wilkinson, S., D. Littlefair and L. Barlow-Meade (2013), 'What is recognised as ability in physical education? A systematic appraisal of how ability and ability differences are socially constructed within mainstream secondary school physical education', *European Physical Education Review*, Vol. 19, 147–164.

World Education Forum (2015), *Incheon Declaration: Education 2030: Towards Inclusive and Equitable Quality Education and Lifelong Learning for All*, available at: https://en.unesco.org/world-education-forum-2015/incheon-declaration

Chapter 8
Achieve Gender Equality and Empower All Women and Girls (SDG 5)

8.1 Introduction

Gender equality is central to the core values and principles of the Commonwealth and to the achievement of sustainable development. In its own right, SDG 5 specifically recognises the importance of gender equality and the empowerment of women and girls. Gender issues are also more broadly acknowledged throughout the *2030 Agenda for Sustainable Development* with particular targets related to women and girls included across a number of goals, including those for SDGs 4, 8, 11 and 16 that are considered in this guide.

Gender equality and empowerment have been a common focus of sport and development policies, including the *Commonwealth Guide to Advancing Development through Sport* (Kay and Dudfield 2013) and the *Declaration of Berlin* (UNESCO 2013), and have been central to specific sport-based initiatives in many countries. However, associated with SDG target 5.1, there remains a significant need to address the gender inequalities evident in sport. It is widely and internationally recognised that gender inequalities in sport participation begin in childhood (Bailey *et al.* 2004; Saavedra 2009; Jeanes *et al.* 2016) and are replicated in global statistics that show that young and adult females are less likely, by six and seven percentage points, respectively, to meet recommended levels of physical activity (WHO 2014) (see Figure 8.1).

There remains a significant need to address the gender inequalities evident in sport.

The relevance of SDG target 5.5, ensuring opportunities for female leadership and decision making, is also demonstrated through globally collected data that show that women are significantly under-represented in national and international leadership roles in sport (Women on Boards 2016). Nevertheless, initiatives that are well designed and targeted can also contribute to this target through facilitating the empowerment of specific groups of women. Such initiatives

Figure 8.1 Inequalities in sport and physical education: Participation in physical activity

Source: WHO (2014)

can also contribute to SDG targets 5.2 and 5.3, which prioritise the elimination of all forms of violence and harmful practices against women and girls. A similar balance must again be employed with vigilance and action to prevent and address such problems where they occur within sport.

Box 8.1 Enhancing the contribution of sport to Sustainable Development Goal 5: Key policy implications

- Priority should be given to addressing gender equality and empowering girls and women, both within and through sport, to contribute to SDG 5.
- Mainstreaming requires the application of a gender-sensitive approach across all policy stages, including formulation, resource allocation, implementation and evaluation.
- Multiple stakeholders need to be engaged to contribute collectively to gender equality across all levels of sport and to integrate approaches across different sectors.
- Recognition of socio-cultural gender norms and their association with sport should inform both scaled and specifically targeted approaches.
- Sport-based approaches can and must engage boys and men in addressing gender equality in and through sport.

8.2 Analysis of sport and specific SDG targets

Target 5.1 End all forms of discrimination against all women and girls everywhere.

Deeply symbiotic relationships exist between discrimination against girls and women within different societies and the reproduction of inequalities within the context of sport. These relationships present significant opportunities and challenges for sport and development. Enhancing equality and equity for girls and women within sport can challenge broader discriminatory norms (Shehu 2010) and, in so doing, strengthen all efforts towards SDG 5. On the other hand, negative stereotypes of girls and women that exist within sport can continue to reinforce embedded cultural values and gender discrimination. Girls' and women's involvement in sport is similarly framed and influenced by structured inequalities that may have both universal and context-specific dimensions (Saavedra 2009).

Enhancing equality and equity for girls and women within sport can challenge broader discriminatory norms and, in so doing, strengthen all efforts towards SDG 5.

Policy development must, therefore, be undertaken in full cognisance of broader discrimination against girls and women, and also be sensitive to context-specific influences on their involvement in sport. Addressing discrimination against women benefits from harnessing the potential of complementarities within and beyond sport. Efforts that involve different stakeholders to improve gender equality at all levels of sport can be mutually reinforcing. Equally, significant improvements can be realised within sport through alignment with wider gender policies and by drawing on the expertise of government departments and other agencies responsible for women's affairs and gender equality. Addressing the societal and structural change required to address all forms of discrimination against girls and women is, however, a long-term process, and so sport-related policy aspirations must be realistically framed (United Nations 2007).

Addressing discrimination against women and girls in sport requires balanced policy approaches that both embed gender equality within all practices and enable specific and targeted actions where appropriate (Chawansky 2011). Mainstreaming gender equality throughout all policy processes benefits from well-developed systems of information gathering, communication and accountability. Collation and dissemination of gender-disaggregated monitoring of resource allocation and policy implementation, and of other measures of equality in sport,

Addressing discrimination against women and girls in sport requires balanced policy approaches that both embed gender equality within all practices and enable specific and targeted actions where appropriate.

can fulfil important functions – from enforcement of existing legislation to informing particular sport-based initiatives. Such data can also be used effectively to inform capacity-building across a range of sport and development stakeholders, and to shape media strategies and campaigns to address gender inequality.

Care must equally be applied to ensure that girls' and women's participation in separate environments, or in specific sports, does not reinforce social divisions or generate unhelpful resistance from other members of society.

Achieving gender equality also depends on developing appropriate opportunities for the involvement of girls and women in sport. Approaches must address both specific barriers that impede girls' and women's participation in sport and the often complex intersections of gender-specific issues and other markers of disadvantage, such as disability, ethnicity and socio-economic status (Jeanes *et al.* 2016). The provision of competitive and non-competitive sporting activities that are attractive to girls and women also requires intentional planning (Bailey *et al.* 2009). In some contexts, girls and women can benefit from specific opportunities that enable them to participate in environments that are safe and supportive. However, care must equally be applied to ensure that girls' and women's participation in separate environments, or in specific sports, does not reinforce social divisions or generate unhelpful resistance from other members of society (Hayhurst *et al.* 2014). These considerations also point to the importance of adopting decentralised approaches that are sensitive to local cultural norms and engage all family and community members (Kay and Spaaij 2012), including boys and men, even in initiatives that may be specifically targeted at girls and women.

Target 5.5 Ensure women's full and effective participation and equal opportunities for leadership at all levels of decision making in political, economic and public life.

For young females, in particular, leadership experiences gained through sport-based initiatives may make distinctive contributions to their empowerment in other social, economic and political spheres.

Females have commonly and traditionally been significantly under-represented in leadership and decision making at all levels in sport and across local, regional, national and international sporting bodies (Women on Boards 2016) (see Figure 8.2). Addressing this embedded and structured inequality is, therefore, a priority in itself. Importantly, enabling the equal involvement of women, from a diverse range of backgrounds, across the full spectrum of sport leadership roles will also enhance gender sensitivity in policy-making, planning, delivery, monitoring and evaluation, thereby contributing to other SDG 5

Figure 8.2 Inequalities in sport and physical education: Governing boards of international sport

Source: Women on Boards (2016)

targets. For young females, in particular, leadership experiences gained through sport-based initiatives may make distinctive contributions to their empowerment in other social, economic and political spheres (Lindsey *et al.* 2016).

Encouraging and promoting different types of female role models can make varying contributions to these outcomes. The significant profile of some elite female athletes can provide opportunities for advocacy and impetus to address gender inequality. The presentation of sexualised images of female athletes in the media can, however, undermine this platform (Sherry *et al.* 2015). Localised female role models can have an especially strong impact, particularly if they have direct involvement or lines of communication with girls or young women (Meier 2015). Close interaction with female role models whose own position may be seen as attainable can be particularly important in engaging female participants in sport and in building their own leadership skills. Furthermore, given the popularity of sport for boys and men, it can be valuable to enhance, with sensitivity, the contribution that female athletes and role models can offer in challenging dominant gender norms (Meier and Saavedra 2009).

Female leadership and empowerment in sport has been promoted within and by specific initiatives in many contexts. When specifically designed, sport-based programmes can provide a safe environment in which young women, in particular, can develop a range of skills and experiences through involvement in coaching, officiating and a range of other roles (Murray 2016). Such programmes can also be a particularly effective context in which girls and women can build strong and mutually supportive relationships (Kay 2009; Samie *et al.* 2015). For sport programmes that do specifically contribute to the development of young women, it is vital that effective links and appropriate pathways within and beyond sport are created to enable them to utilise fully the leadership skills that have been developed (Hayhurst 2014).

Detailed evidence of gender inequalities in sport leadership, and of opportunities and outcomes being skewed towards men at all levels of sport, can be an important policy tool.

Improving female leadership and participation in decision making requires both a thorough analysis to address existing barriers and a supportive policy environment that enables complementary efforts to be realised. Detailed evidence of gender inequalities in sport leadership, and of opportunities and outcomes being skewed towards men at all levels of sport, can be an important policy tool. This is especially the case given that influence to address gender inequalities needs to be exerted across public, non-profit, commercial and media stakeholders in sport. Specific initiatives can make important contributions to enabling female leadership and decision making in sport, but these also benefit from linking into broader policies and partnerships with organisations working specifically on gender issues. It is through such collective approaches that systematic change for all women and girls can be promoted (Ferkins and Broadbent 2009).

Target 5.2 Eliminate all forms of violence against all women and girls in the public and private spheres, including trafficking and sexual and other types of exploitation.

Target 5.3 Eliminate all harmful practices, such as child, early and forced marriage, and female genital mutilation.

Societal problems of violence and abuse have been and are reproduced in sport.

As with each SDG 5 target, efforts both within and through sport can support the goal of eliminating all forms of violence and harmful practices against girls and women. Societal problems of violence and abuse have been and are reproduced in sport. Young females can be especially vulnerable if coaches and administrators abuse their positions of trust and responsibility (Kerr and Stirling 2008; Lang and Hartill 2014). In contexts in which sport may be considered as a masculine domain, girls and women may be exposed to increased risk merely through their visible participation in sport (Jeanes and Magee 2014). Under SDG 16, further attention is given to the increasing impetus that international policy gives to raising awareness of these problems and to promoting approaches to safeguard all children in sport. Ensuring that girls and women are not subject to any form of violence or harm within sport also requires continued efforts to change dominant masculine cultures where they exist in sport, the creation and maintenance of safe spaces for participation by girls and women (see SDG 11), and ongoing vigilance on the part of all stakeholders.

Sport can also make distinctive contributions to these targets through intentionally planned and well-delivered initiatives. Specific programming and activities can build awareness and understanding of various issues, including sexual health, gender-based violence and other harmful practices (Hershow *et al.* 2015). Peer education approaches have also been utilised in sport to provide supportive environments for discussion of gender-related issues, and to enable the empowerment of girls and young women. Sport may also provide a particularly appropriate environment through which boys and men can be sensitised to issues of gender equality and co-opted into proactive advocacy (Larkin *et al.* 2007; Chawansky 2011). Ensuring that all such initiatives are appropriately designed to take account of specific cultural contexts is vital. Furthermore, given the sensitivities involved, it is essential that all those involved in the delivery of activities have appropriate knowledge and skills, and have access to additional training and support where necessary.

Specific programming and activities can build awareness and understanding of various issues, including sexual health, gender-based violence and other harmful practices.

Broader actions may also be important for encouraging and enabling stakeholders associated with sport to maximise their contributions to SDG targets 5.2 and 5.3. There needs to be sustained emphasis within forums for sport policy-making on the elimination of violence and harmful practices, and implementation at all levels. Building awareness and capacity across all organisations and individuals involved in sport is also essential. Beyond targeted information campaigns, scaled impact can be achieved through mainstreaming gender issues

The *Girls Make Your Move* campaign: Inspiring, energising and empowering young women to be more active

Lachlan Cameron
Office for Sport, Department of Health
Government of Australia

Physical inactivity is the second greatest contributor to the cancer burden in Australia and the leading contributor to preventable illness and morbidity among women (ABS 2013).

According to the Australian Health Survey (2011–12), nine in ten young Australians don't move enough. Physical activity decreases with age, with a clear turning point identified in the late teen years–a time when establishing healthy and active lifestyle choices is important. Further to this, young women experience unique barriers that deter them from being as physically active as young men, including self-consciousness and a fear of being judged.

Launched in February 2016, Australia's *Girls Make Your Move* behaviour change campaign works to inspire, energise and empower young women and girls aged 12–19 to be more active. Alongside wider initiatives to encourage young people's participation in physical activity and sport, it addresses perceived barriers and generates positive perceptions, pitching physical activity and sport as fun, healthy and social.

The campaign targets those who are less skilled and passionate but still enjoy activity, as well as those who were formerly active but whose participation has dropped off as a result of other commitments. The aim is to re-engage them by demonstrating a wide range of non-sport activities and the social benefits of being active.

It also involves parents, recognising their influence on reinforcing physical activity by providing support, being active themselves and encouraging family activity.

The campaign comprises television, online and print media, and out-of home advertising and public relations. It is the first Australian Federal Government campaign to have used Facebook canvas advertising and social media influencers to drive and encourage behaviour change. The advertising is supported by a programme of events, a website and an Instagram presence with over 7,000 followers to engage with young women and encourage them to 'find their thing'. Engagement across these media platforms responds to SDG Target 5.b which aims to enhance the use of enabling technology to promote the empowerment of women.

Girls Make Your Move was inspired by the UK's *This Girl Can*, but was produced for a younger audience in the Australian context. It has been assessed as highly novel, captivating and atypical of traditional government advertising. The target audience has welcomed the coverage of a range of young women enjoying different activities in a non-competitive, judgemental or prescriptive way.

(Continued)

The *Girls Make Your Move* campaign: Inspiring, energising and empowering young women to be more active (*cont.*)

The campaign has reached over 80 per cent of girls aged 12–19 years across the nation. Independent evaluation results show that the campaign's impact on attitudes and intentions has been overwhelmingly positive. One in four girls surveyed reported having interacted with the campaign's social media activities, and one in five reported doing more physical activity as a result (Australian Government, Department of Health, 2016). The initiative contributes to achieving SDG target 3.4, which aims to reduce premature mortality from non-communicable disease.

Overall, the campaign has been found to be wide-reaching, engaging, motivating and empowering, which points to its effectiveness. It has broad appeal to female audiences and is suitable for adaptation for countries facing similar trends.

The *Girls Make Your Move* campaign contributes in particular to the following SDGs:

SDG3 Ensure healthy lives and promote well-being for all, at all ages

SDG5 Achieve gender equality and empower all women and girls.

within coach education and sport administrator training (Swiss Agency for Development and Cooperation 2005; Pfister 2010). Associated with SDG 16, governance systems for sport also need to be fully accountable in addressing issues of gender-based violence and harmful practices, in order to command the confidence of all girls and women involved in sport.

8.3 The means of implementation: Policy options for Sustainable Development Goal 5

Policy development must seek to improve gender equality within sport and also utilise opportunities for gender empowerment through sport. The scale of the gender equity issues associated with sport calls for strong enactment of a range of policy options. These options include recourse to wider systems of regulation and involve gender-sensitive systems of funding distribution and re-distribution, and various approaches to data and information gathering and dissemination that build awareness and ensure accountability. Decision making regarding the use and implementation of policy options must be sensitive to specific socio-cultural complexities that present particular opportunities and challenges for gender equality.

Policy development must seek to improve gender equality within sport and also utilise opportunities for gender empowerment through sport.

Table 8.1 Policy options to enhance the contribution of sport to SDG 5

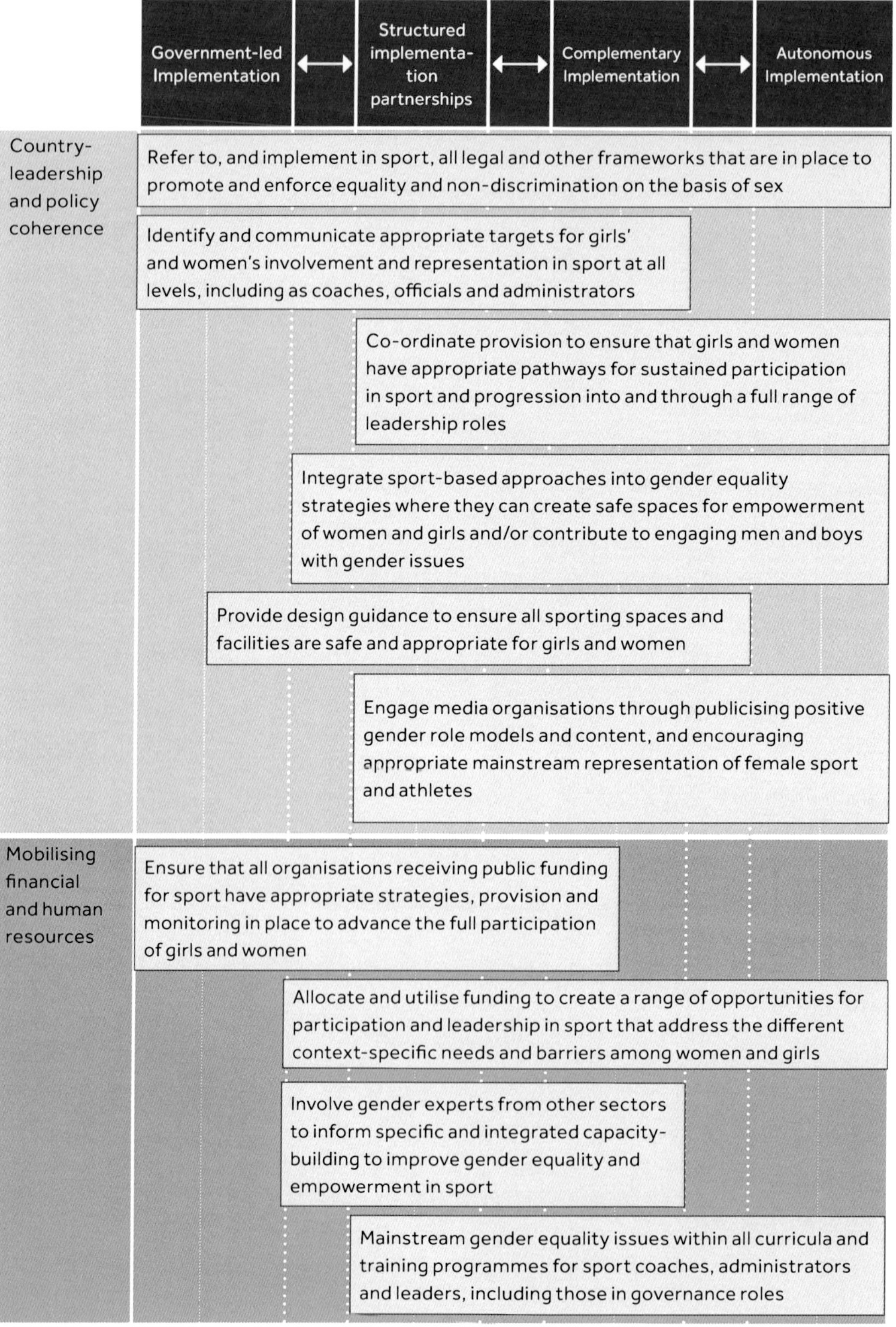

	Government-led Implementation ⟷ Structured implementation partnerships ⟷ Complementary Implementation ⟷ Autonomous Implementation
Country-leadership and policy coherence	Refer to, and implement in sport, all legal and other frameworks that are in place to promote and enforce equality and non-discrimination on the basis of sex
	Identify and communicate appropriate targets for girls' and women's involvement and representation in sport at all levels, including as coaches, officials and administrators
	Co-ordinate provision to ensure that girls and women have appropriate pathways for sustained participation in sport and progression into and through a full range of leadership roles
	Integrate sport-based approaches into gender equality strategies where they can create safe spaces for empowerment of women and girls and/or contribute to engaging men and boys with gender issues
	Provide design guidance to ensure all sporting spaces and facilities are safe and appropriate for girls and women
	Engage media organisations through publicising positive gender role models and content, and encouraging appropriate mainstream representation of female sport and athletes
Mobilising financial and human resources	Ensure that all organisations receiving public funding for sport have appropriate strategies, provision and monitoring in place to advance the full participation of girls and women
	Allocate and utilise funding to create a range of opportunities for participation and leadership in sport that address the different context-specific needs and barriers among women and girls
	Involve gender experts from other sectors to inform specific and integrated capacity-building to improve gender equality and empowerment in sport
	Mainstream gender equality issues within all curricula and training programmes for sport coaches, administrators and leaders, including those in governance roles

(Continued)

Table 8.1 Policy options to enhance the contribution of sport to SDG 5 (*cont.*)

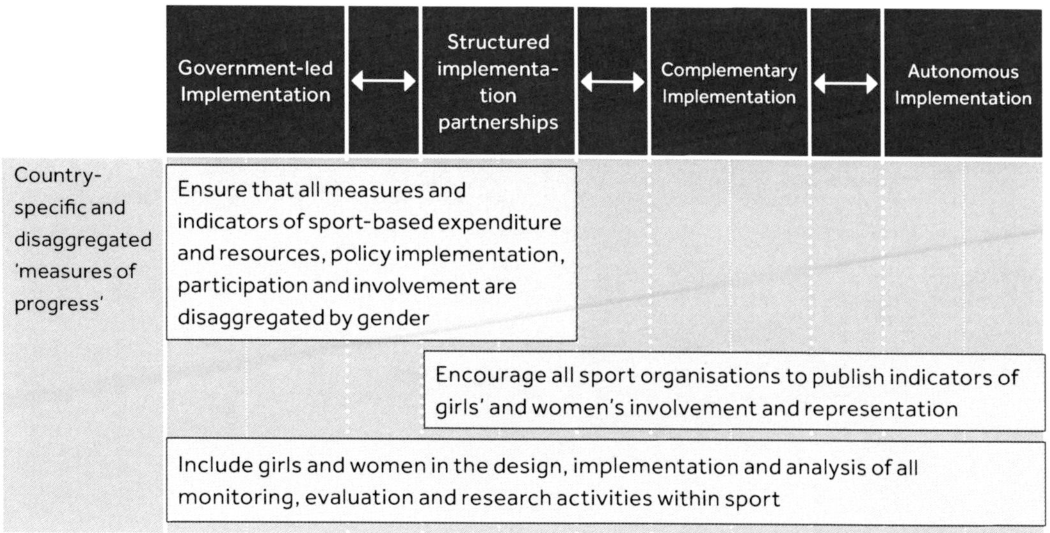

	Government-led Implementation	Structured implementation partnerships	Complementary Implementation	Autonomous Implementation
Country-specific and disaggregated 'measures of progress'	Ensure that all measures and indicators of sport-based expenditure and resources, policy implementation, participation and involvement are disaggregated by gender			
		Encourage all sport organisations to publish indicators of girls' and women's involvement and representation		
	Include girls and women in the design, implementation and analysis of all monitoring, evaluation and research activities within sport			

References

Australian Bureau of Statistics (ABS) (2013), *Australian Health Survey: First Results, 2011-12*, ABS Cat. No. 4364.0.55.001, Canberra, ABS.

Australian Government, Department of Health (2016), *Campaign Evaluation: Girls Make Your Move*, available at: http://www.health.gov.au/internet/girlsmove/publishing.nsf/Content/evaluation

Bailey, R., K. Armour, D. Kirk, M. Jess, I. Pickup and R. Sandford (2009), 'The educational benefits claimed for physical education and school sport: an academic review', *Research Papers in Education*, Vol. 24, 1–27.

Bailey, R., I. Wellard and H. Dismore (2004), *Girls' Participation in Physical Activities and Sports: Benefits, Patterns, Influences and Ways Forward*, World Health Organization, Geneva.

Chawansky, M. (2011), 'New social movements, old gender games? Locating girls in the sport for development and peace movement', *Research in Social Movements, Conflicts and Change*, Vol. 32, 121–134.

Ferkins, L. and S. Broadbent (2009), *Women in Sport Leadership: The Missing Dimension, International Evidence for Change*, available at: http://dro.deakin.edu.au/eserv/DU:30020734/ferkins-womeninsport-2009.pdf

Hayhurst, L. M. (2014), 'The "Girl Effect" and martial arts: social entrepreneurship and sport, gender and development in Uganda', *Gender, Place & Culture*, Vol. 21, 297–315.

Hayhurst, L. M., M. MacNeill, B. Kidd and A. Knoppers (2014), 'Gender relations, gender-based violence and sport for development and peace: Questions, concerns and cautions emerging from Uganda', *Women's Studies International Forum*, Vol. 47, 157–167.

Hershow, R. B., K. Gannett, J. Merrill, B. E. Kaufman, C. Barkley, J. DeCelles and A. Harrison (2015), 'Using soccer to build confidence and increase HCT uptake among adolescent girls: a mixed-methods study of an HIV prevention programme in South Africa', *Sport in Society*, Vol. 18, 1009–1022.

Jeanes, R. and J. D. Magee, (2014), 'Promoting gender empowerment through sport? Exploring the experiences of Zambian female footballers', in

Schulenkorf, N. and D. Adair (Eds) *Global Sport-For-Development: Critical Perspectives*, Palgrave Macmillan, London, 134–154.

Jeanes, R., L. Hills and T. Kay (2016), 'Women, sport and gender inequity', in Houlihan, B. and D. Malcolm (Eds), *Sport and Society* (3rd ed.), Sage, London, 134–156.

Kay, T. (2009), 'Developing through sport: Evidencing social impacts on young people', *Sport in Society*, Vol. 12, 1177–1191.

Kay, T. and O. Dudfield (2013), *The Commonwealth Guide to Advancing Development through Sport*, Commonwealth Secretariat, London, available at: http://assets.thecommonwealth.org/assetbank-commonwealth/action/viewAsset?id=23162andindex=3andtotal=11andview=viewSearchItem

Kay, T. and R. Spaaij (2012), 'The mediating effects of family on sport in international development contexts', *International Review for the Sociology of Sport*, Vol. 47, 77–94.

Kerr, G. A. and A. E. Stirling (2008), 'Child protection in sport: Implications of an athlete-centred philosophy', *Quest*, 60 (2), 307–323.

Lang, M. and M. Hartill (2014), *Safeguarding, Child Protection and Abuse in Sport: International Perspectives in Research, Policy and Practice*, Routledge, Abingdon.

Larkin, J., S. Razack and F. Moola (2007), 'Gender, Sport and Development', in Kidd, B. and P. Donnelly (Eds), *Literature Reviews on Sport for Development and Peace*, available at: http://www.righttoplay.com/moreinfo/aboutus/Documents/Literature%20Reviews%20SDP.pdf#search=literature%20reviews

Lindsey, I., T. Kay, R. Jeanes and D. Banda (2016), *Localizing Global Sport for Development*, Manchester University Press, Manchester.

Meier, M. (2015), 'The value of female sporting role models', *Sport in Society*, Vol. 18, 968–982.

Meier, M. and M. Saavedra (2009), 'Esther Phiri and the Moutawakel effect in Zambia: an analysis of the use of female role models in sport-for-development', *Sport in Society*, Vol. 12, 1158–1176.

Murray, S. (2016), 'Reflection on Beyond Girl Power and the Girl Effect: The Girling of Sport for Development and Peace', in Hayhurst, L. M. C., T. Kay and M. Chawansky (Eds), *Beyond Sport for Development and Peace: Transnational Perspectives on Theory, Policy and Practice*, Routledge, Abingdon, 106–110.

Pfister, G. (2010), 'Women in sport: Gender relations and future perspectives', *Sport in Society*, Vol. 13, 234–248.

Saavedra, M. (2009), 'Dilemmas and opportunities in gender and sport in development', in Levermore, R. and A. Beacom (Eds), *Sport and International Development*, Palgrave Macmillan, Basingstoke, 124–155.

Samie, S. F., A. J. Johnson, A. M. Huffman and S. J. Hillyer (2015), 'Voices of empowerment: women from the Global South re/negotiating empowerment and the global sports mentoring programme', *Sport in Society*, Vol. 18, 923–937.

Shehu, J. (Ed.) (2010), *Gender, Sport, and Development in Africa: Cross-cultural Perspectives on Patterns of Representations and Marginalization*, Codesria, Senegal.

Sherry, E., A. Osborne and M. Nicholson (2015), 'Images of sports women: a review', *Sex Roles*, Vol. 74, 299–309.

Swiss Agency for Development and Cooperation (2005), *Gender and Sport: Mainstreaming Gender in Sports Projects*, available at: http://www.bridge.ids.ac.uk/sites/bridge.ids.ac.uk/files/Docs/Sport_englisch.pdf

UNESCO (2013), *Declaration of Berlin*, available at: http://unesdoc.unesco.org/images/0022/002211/221114e.pdf

United Nations (2007), *Women, Gender Equality and Sport*, available at: http://www.un.org/womenwatch/daw/public/Women%20and%20Sport.pdf

Women on Boards (2016), 'Gender Balance in Global Sport Report', available at: https://www.womenonboards.net/womenonboards-AU/media/AU-Reports/2016-Gender-Balance-In-Global-Sport-Report.pdf

World Health Organization (WHO) (2014), *Global Status Report on Non-communicable Diseases 2014*, available at: http://www.who.int/nmh/publications/ncd-status-report-2014/en/

Chapter 9
Promote Sustained, Inclusive and Sustainable Economic Growth, Full and Productive Employment and Decent Work for All (SDG 8)

9.1 Introduction

The Millennium Development Goal (MDG) target of halving the proportion of people living in extreme poverty was met five years ahead of schedule. Overall, the number of people living on less than US$1.25 per day fell from 1.9 billion in 1990 to 836 million in 2015 (United Nations 2015). While SDGs 1 and 10 represent a continued focus on poverty and all aspects of inequality, SDG 8 gives broader attention to 'sustained, inclusive and sustainable growth' as a foundation for prosperity and sustainable development more generally.

SDG 8 also continues to prioritise 'full and productive employment and decent work for all', an aspiration for which there has been a lack of progress since its inclusion in the MDGs. Globally, the proportion of the working-age population who are employed has fallen, and the 204 million people who were unemployed in 2015 represented a significant increase both from 1991 and since the 2008 global economic crisis (United Nations 2015). The International Labour Organization (ILO) has identified that young people, and especially young women, across the globe have been significantly and particularly affected by a 'prolonged job crisis'. Globally, estimated figures for youth unemployment stood at 12.6 per cent in 2013, with as many as 73 million young people being without work (ILO 2013). Youth unemployment and underemployment are especially acute in developing regions, where particular problems with the quality, stability and regularity of work are recognised (ILO 2013).

The potential for sport to contribute to SDG 8 is connected to recognition by the World Economic Forum's Global Agenda Council on the Role of Sports in Society that it has become 'one of the top ten industries globally (that) has truly achieved a global presence (and) is uniquely placed to provide long-lasting effects that support economic growth' (World Economic Forum 2009). Moreover, progress towards other SDGs could also have a broader economic impact. For example, increases in sport-based participation associated with SDG 3 can reduce the direct and indirect costs of physical inactivity, which are projected to reach US$7.5 billion and US$26 billion in India and the United Kingdom, respectively, by 2030.

In relation to SDG targets 8.1 and 8.9, it is especially important to recognise the varied economic activity that may be generated at different levels of sport and in different country contexts through participant and spectator costs; facility construction; equipment and clothing manufacturing; media and sponsorship; and events, travel and tourism. Employment in all of these areas can contribute to SDG target 8.5, and the particular properties of sport make it suitable for contributing to SDG targets 8.3 and 8.6 – associated entrepreneurship and youth unemployment, respectively. However, concerns with regard to labour rights and migration within the sport industry means that attention must also be given to SDG targets 8.7 and 8.8.

Box 9.1 Enhancing the contribution of sport to Sustainable Development Goal 8: Key policy implications

- The sport industry may make a valuable contribution to economic growth and employment, but capacity-building for the collection of precise data on the scale of this impact is required in many countries.
- Place-based sport event and tourism policies have been particularly prominent in seeking to derive economic benefits from sport.
- Sport-based approaches to employment training, entrepreneurship and enterprise have emerged and need to take account of opportunities within the broader economy to maximise their potential.
- Strategic planning is required to leverage economic benefits through sport and to link sport-based approaches to potential job markets.
- Policy-makers have responsibility for ensuring that labour rights are enforced within and around sport, particularly for employees in sports construction and manufacturing and for young people seeking careers in professional sport.

9.2 Analysis of sport and specific SDG targets

Target 8.1 Sustain per capita economic growth in accordance with national circumstances and, in particular, at least 7 per cent GDP growth per annum in the least developed countries.

Target 8.9 By 2030, devise and implement policies to promote sustainable tourism that creates jobs and promotes local culture and products.

Findings have pointed to the growing economic value of sport while also indicating the financial value derived from sport-based interventions that deliver social benefit.

Informed economic policy-making related to sport requires measurement of the value of the sport industry. The complexities associated with the collection of such data are magnified when recognition is given to the diverse range of economic activities that are directly and indirectly associated with sport. In countries where there are expertise and available data to undertake such economic analysis, findings have pointed to the growing economic value of sport while also indicating the financial value derived from sport-based interventions that deliver social benefit (Crabbe 2013; Fujiwara *et al.* 2014). Indeed, one global estimate puts the value of the entire sport industry at US$700 billion per annum, a figure that represents 1 per cent of global GDP (Kearney 2014). Taxation from sport commonly exceeds sport-related government expenditure, and the economic scale of professional sport has increased rapidly in many countries (Gratton *et al.* 2012). There are, however, significant variations in national access to, and expertise for, economic analyses of sport, with constraints in low- and medium-income countries being particularly acute. Even in high-income Commonwealth countries, there can be concerns about the reliability of estimates and data at sub-national and local levels (Davies 2010).

These limitations are especially pertinent because of the policy impetus to promote sport-based economic activity, and impact has often centred on place-based and event-oriented approaches. Significant claims have been made for the economic impact of major sport events. For example, the Durban Commonwealth Games in 2022 are predicted to generate economic impact worth £502 million (Ernst and Young 2014). However, strategies for bidding and hosting major sport events must be developed and pursued with care; the evidence for the economic benefits of major sport events is not unequivocal (Gratton *et al.* 2012), and pre-event predictions of economic impact have commonly been far greater than post-event analysis has found (Kasamati 2008). Concerns have also been raised about the relative distribution of economic benefits, both geographically within countries and across sections of the population (Cornelissen 2009).

While there has been an increasing trend for some developing countries to bid for and host major sport events, this is not a viable strategy for many Commonwealth countries. However, there has been growing interest in hosting the increasing range of smaller, so-called non-mega sport events. Hosting such events may be more feasible in many contexts, as they may not involve the construction or renovation of facilities, and other related infrastructure requirements are less onerous (Agha and Taks 2015). Reduced infrastructure costs may make non-mega sport events a better policy approach for achieving optimal economic impact (Taks 2016; Gibson *et al.* 2012), although there remains a need for further rigorous analysis of such claims.

Smaller non-mega sport events may represent a more optimal policy approach to achieve economic impact from hosting sporting events.

Promotion of place-based sport tourism can also contribute to economic impact and can take a variety of different forms. A high profile has been accorded to spectator tourism linked to hosting of sport events. Given the variety of different events and hosts, conclusive evidence of their economic impact is not available. Major and smaller-scale events can have different impacts in respect of the quantity of incoming spectators and the extent to which these may crowd out other tourist visits and spending (Gibson *et al.* 2012; Taks 2016). Consideration also needs to be given to the potential of sport events to improve the international image of cities and as a stimulus to develop tourism infrastructure (Gratton *et al.* 2012).

Sport tourism opportunities also include those based on more active forms of participation. In this regard, sport can be either the sole reason for tourism or an important factor that influences tourists' choice of destinations. Different locations may be better suited to single- or multi-sport tourism, but opportunities for sporting activity can often be included effectively in place-based tourism marketing (Hinch and Higham 2008). All approaches to garnering economic impact through sport tourism may be best realised through drawing on capacities across public–private and civil society partnerships (see Figure 9.1).

Sport can be either the sole reason for tourism or an important factor that influences tourists' choice of destinations.

Overall, enhancing the economic impact of sport through place-based and event-oriented approaches requires strategic planning

Figure 9.1 Enhancing the economic impact of sport through place-based and event-orientated tourism

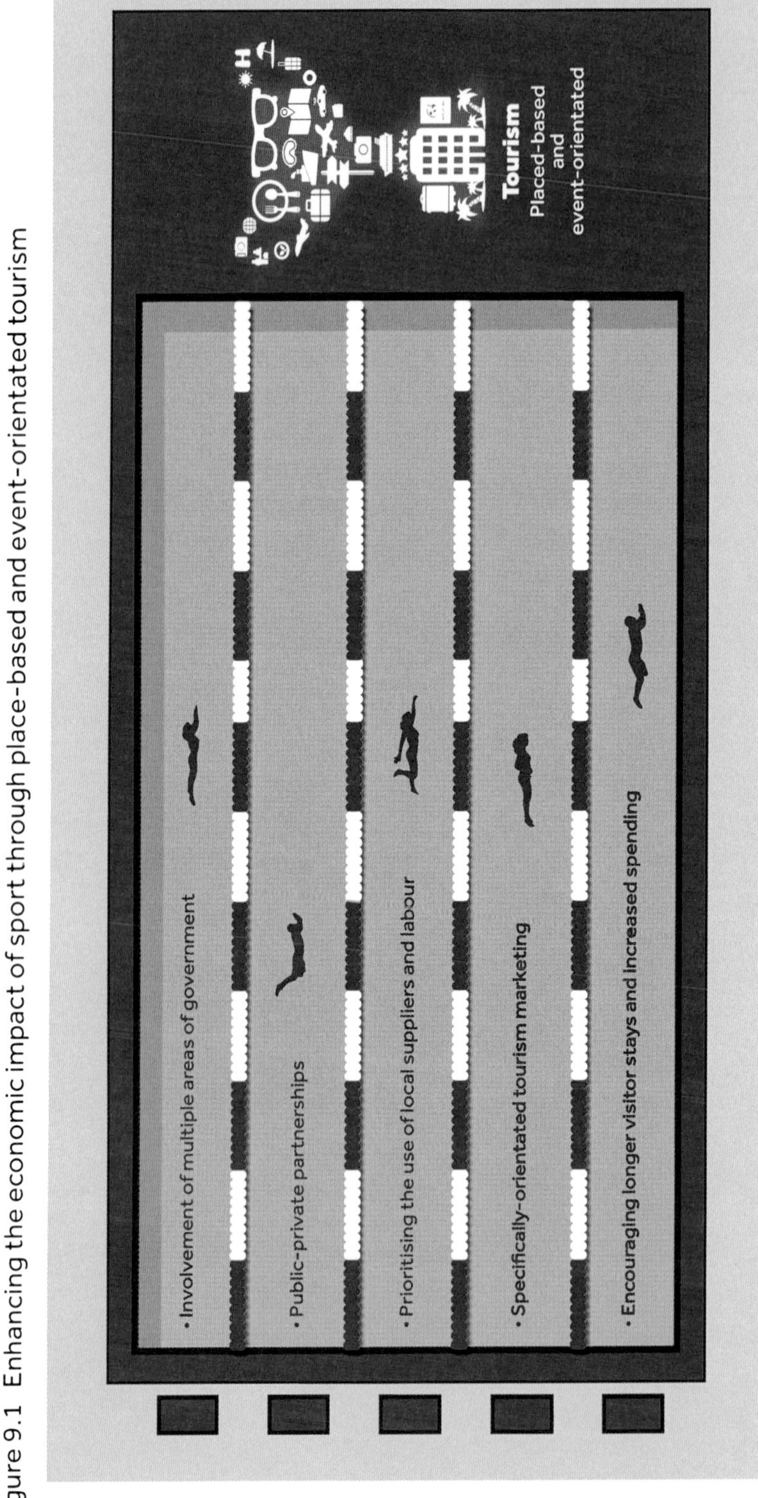

Source: Kasamati (2008); Cornelissen (2009); Challip and Heere (2014)

and implementation that is co-ordinated across the sectors of national and local government responsible for economic development, infrastructure and regeneration, as well as tourism and sport. There is evidence that long-term incremental strategies for sport-based economic development, which may culminate in the hosting of major events, can be particularly productive and enable greater alignment with the principles of sustainable development (Kasamati 2008; Cornelissen 2009). Regardless, strategies must seek to leverage maximum economic benefit through public–private partnerships, prioritising the use of local suppliers and labour, developing specifically oriented tourism marketing, and encouraging longer visitor stays and increased spending (Challip and Heere 2014).

There is evidence that long-term incremental strategies for sport-based economic development, which may culminate in the hosting of major events, can be particularly productive and enable greater alignment with the principles of sustainable development.

Target 8.5 By 2030, achieve full and productive employment and decent work for all women and men, including for young people and persons with disabilities, and equal pay for work of equal value.

Target 8.3 Promote development-oriented policies that support productive activities, decent job creation, entrepreneurship, creativity and innovation, and encourage the formalisation and growth of micro-, small- and medium-sized enterprises, including through access to financial services.

Target 8.6 By 2020, substantially reduce the proportion of youth not in employment, education or training.

Data on trends in employment within sport are more limited than for overall sport-based economic activity. However, some analyses point to concerns that secure, long-term employment may not be the norm in some parts of the sport industry (Camy 2006; Primault 2006), although progress has been made in particular countries towards professionalising some sport-related jobs. Some indicators also point to a high proportion of part-time jobs within the sport industry (Camy 2006).

Permeable boundaries between volunteering and paid employment in sport can bring the potential for exploitation (Primault 2006). Nevertheless, the strong culture of volunteering in sport brings many benefits. Where calculated (Australian Sports Commission 2010), the economic value of sport-based volunteering is significant and, for individuals, volunteering in sport can provide accessible routes into paid employment. Participation and, especially, volunteering in

The strong culture of volunteering in sport brings many benefits.

sport can contribute to the development of core skills such as communication, teamwork and problem solving. As recognised by the Organisation for Economic Co-operation and Development (OECD) and the ILO, using the popularity of sport as an engagement tool can enhance policies and practices that seek to address the priority of youth unemployment through working with those who have not attended or completed school (ILO 2013).

Education and training towards employability has been an integral part of a number of sport-based initiatives.

Education and training towards employability has been an integral part of a number of sport-based initiatives. For example, initiatives associated with the Glasgow 2014 Commonwealth Games provided specifically targeted training and opportunities to support young or previously unemployed people into work (Commonwealth Games Federation 2014). Across other Commonwealth countries, similar sport-based initiatives have varied in both scale and duration, and have sought to enable employment across a range of industries beyond, and in, sport. It is therefore vital to ensure that participants and volunteers in such initiatives gain technical, job-specific skills and qualifications in addition to other generic and transferable skills. This requires sport-based initiatives to be oriented towards current and future opportunities in identifiable job markets beyond sport and to complement actions by employers and training providers in other industries.

Sport-based approaches that are specifically focused on entrepreneurship and enterprise have gained increasing prominence and can be a source of both social and economic value (Ratten 2011). Sport-based NGOs and other types of civil society organisations have developed different models of entrepreneurial practice and development, including:

- the creation, marketing and sale of innovative sport-based products and services, which may also include distinctive and ethical models of employment or procurement
- the initiation of business enterprises to generate funding to deliver sport-based initiatives and thereby increase sustainability and reduce dependency on external donors
- the provision of specific education and training to develop entrepreneurial skills or enterprise opportunities for participants in sport-based initiatives.

Sport-based approaches may have particular value as they can support the development of collective approaches and networking that can enable entrepreneurship and enterprise, especially in developing countries (Ratten 2014). Examples from Commonwealth countries whereby young females have used sport-based skills to develop their own income-generating activities may be particularly relevant, given that degrees of economic self-sufficiency may be important in addressing female empowerment more generally (Hayhurst 2014).

Again, these agendas are best pursued through cross-sectoral approaches, as recognised in the joint Commonwealth Secretariat and United Nations Conference on Trade and Development (UNCTAD) *Policy Guide on Youth Entrepreneurship* (Commonwealth Secretariat and UNCTAD [n.d.]). Sport-based approaches can benefit from integration with relevant developments and policy in other sectors, not least to improve understanding about effective practices and contextual enablers for entrepreneurship and enterprise (ILO 2013). Access to finance for small- and medium-sized enterprises is a widespread problem, especially in developing countries, but care must also be taken to minimise risks that external funding can contribute to pressure for unsustainable expansion (UNESCO 2013). More generally, broader progress towards good governance and reducing bureaucracy is important for removing potential barriers to entrepreneurship and enterprise (Ratten 2014).

Target 8.8 Protect labour rights and promote safe and secure working environments for all workers, including migrant workers, in particular women migrants, and those in precarious employment.

Target 8.7 Take immediate and effective measures to eradicate forced labour, end modern slavery and human trafficking, and secure the prohibition and elimination of the worst forms of child labour, including recruitment and use of child soldiers, and by 2025 end child labour in all its forms.

The need to institute and effectively implement measures to protect workers is emphasised, as exploitation is increasingly recognised in some parts of the sport industry, especially in areas that have been transformed by globalisation. Opportunities for employment and economic development in low- and medium-income countries have resulted from the widespread outsourcing of sport manufacturing by transnational companies and in the construction of sport stadiums and

Exploitation is increasingly recognised in some parts of the sport industry, especially in areas that have been transformed by globalisation.

infrastructure for the hosting of major events. However, ongoing and multiple concerns have been raised about employment practices, pay and conditions for local and migrant workers in different countries in both of these sectors (Cottle and Rombaldi 2014).

If there is potential for exploitation, national governments bear a particular responsibility for ensuring that international standards for human and workers' rights are adhered to.

If there is potential for exploitation, national governments bear a particular responsibility for ensuring that international standards for human and workers' rights are adhered to. Further intervention may be required in cases where self-regulation enacted through private sector manufacturing supply chains proves ineffective (Thibault 2009). Ensuring recognition of trade unions and working with other civil society networks for workers' rights has also proved to be important in identifying and addressing abuses where they occur (Giulianotti 2011).

The rights of young people seeking careers in professional sport also need to be protected, especially given the increasing number of 'academies' in developing countries that may purport to offer local and global pathways into such employment (Akindes and Kirwan 2009). Potential for exploitation exists because careers in professional sport are achievable for only very few young people, but are highly attractive to many. There is evidence of different standards of ethical practice among academies (Darby 2012), and there are some cases of young people spending significant sums to pursue opportunities sold under false pretences. A more general risk is that the pursuit of professional sport careers may divert young people from alternative education and employment routes.

Some academies have developed innovative models that integrate education and sport development activities and offer dual-career preparation for young people.

There is also diversity in the legal status of academies, especially within and across developing countries (Darby *et al.* 2007). Within the scope of governmental intervention allowed by the statutes of the IOC, FIFA (Fédération Internationale de Football Association) and other international sport federations, there are examples where national agencies have sought to identify and classify all academies, and this offers a route towards adherence with relevant laws and legislation, and integration into regulated sport development structures and systems. There may, therefore, also be scope to encourage the spread of existing examples of good practice, especially as some academies have developed innovative models that integrate education and sport development activities and offer dual-career preparation for young people (Darby 2013).

9.3 The means of implementation: Policy options for Sustainable Development Goal 8

Both national-level economic policy and more targeted implementation can be important in enhancing and ensuring the contribution of sport to SDG 8. This reflects the breadth of possibilities associated with sport, ranging from economic growth within the sport industry to utilising sport-based approaches to enhance wider agendas of employability, entrepreneurism and enterprise. As a result, a range of policy instruments may be usefully employed by policy-makers. Fiscal instruments and investment can directly and indirectly stimulate sport-based economic development. Further development of organisational links between stakeholders across sport and other industries, and providing regulation to protect labour rights and address exploitation, may be appropriate in particular cases. Finally, evidence-based policy-making requires improved data to indicate the scale of, and prospects for, economic development in different sectors of the sport industry.

Evidence-based policy-making requires improved data to indicate the scale of, and prospects for, economic development in different sectors of the sport industry.

Table 9.1 Policy options to enhance the contribution of sport to SDG 8

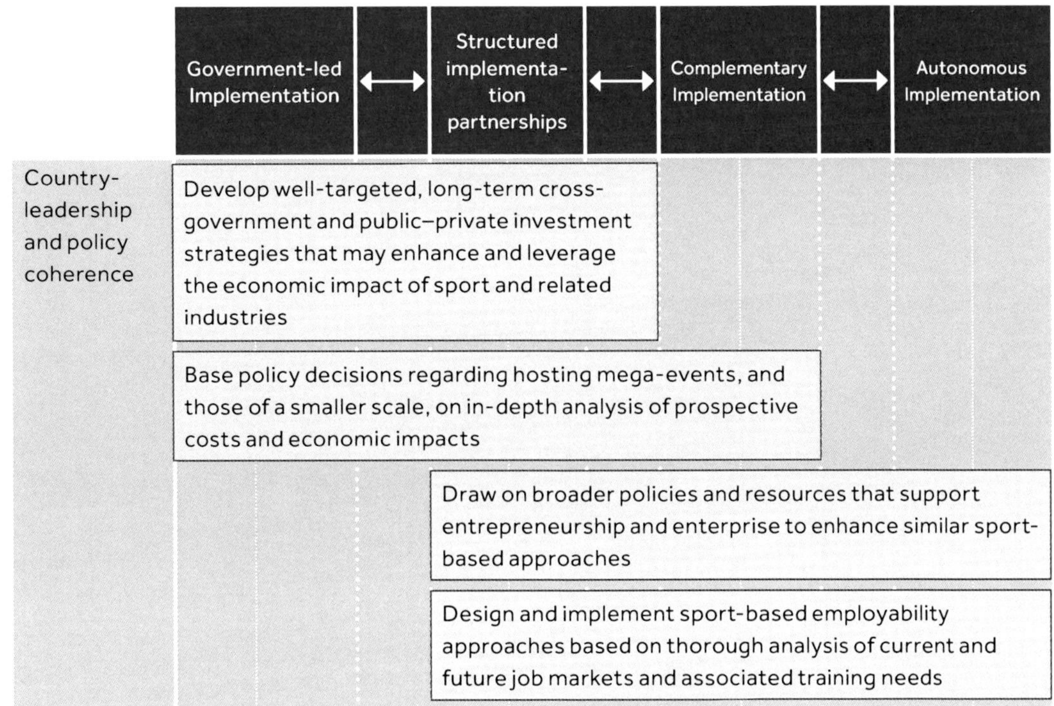

	Government-led Implementation	⟷	Structured implementa-tion partnerships	⟷	Complementary Implementation	⟷	Autonomous Implementation
Country-leadership and policy coherence	Develop well-targeted, long-term cross-government and public–private investment strategies that may enhance and leverage the economic impact of sport and related industries						
	Base policy decisions regarding hosting mega-events, and those of a smaller scale, on in-depth analysis of prospective costs and economic impacts						
			Draw on broader policies and resources that support entrepreneurship and enterprise to enhance similar sport-based approaches				
			Design and implement sport-based employability approaches based on thorough analysis of current and future job markets and associated training needs				

(Continued)

Table 9.1 Policy options to enhance the contribution of sport to SDG 8 (*cont.*)

	Government-led Implementation	⟷	Structured implementa-tion partnerships	⟷	Complementary Implementation	⟷	Autonomous Implementation
Mobilising financial and human resources	Use available fiscal policy instruments to support local supply chains to provide goods and services required at all levels of sport						
	Leverage resources for investment in sport-based approaches through cross-sectoral engagement across sport, tourism, infrastructure, regeneration and economic development						
		Support solidarity in sport through influencing and supporting professional sport to pool and best utilise a proportion of their financial resources in support of grass-roots sport and other sport-based approaches					
		Utilise specific expertise in broader tourism sectors to promote and develop sport-based tourism opportunities					
Country-specific and disaggregated 'measures of progress'	Develop systems to monitor and share good practice and, where appropriate, intervene to protect labour rights across those sectors of the sports industry where problematic practices may be identified						
	Draw on international expertise to enhance national capacity for differentiated analyses of the economic value of all aspects of the sport industry, including that from sport-based employment and volunteering						
					Apply appropriate methodologies to estimate the economic return generated by various and particular types of sport-based initiative		

References

Agha, N. and M. Taks (2015), 'A theoretical comparison of the economic impact of large and small events', *International Journal of Sport Finance*, Vol. 10, 199–216.

Akindes, G. and M. Kirwan (2009), 'Sport as international aid: Assisting development or promoting under-development in Sub-Saharan Africa?', in

Levermore, R. and A. Beacom (Eds), *Sport and International Development*, Macmillan, Basingtoke, 215–245.

Australian Sports Commission (2010), *The Economic Contribution of Sport to Australia*, available at: http://www.ausport.gov.au/__data/assets/pdf_file/0017/341072/Frontier_Research_The_Economic_Contribution_of_Sport_summary_report.pdf

Camy, J. (2006), 'Employment opportunities in the sports sector: A review of the European situation', in di Cola, G. (Ed.), *Beyond the Scoreboard: Youth Employment Opportunities and Skills Development in the Sports Sector*, available at: http://www.ilo.org/wcmsp5/groups/public/---ed_emp/documents/publication/wcms_116484.pdf

Challip, L. and B. Heere (2014), 'Leveraging Sports Events; Fundamentals and application to bids', in Henry, I. and L. M. Ko (Eds), *Handbook of Sport Policy*, Routledge, Abingdon, 183–194.

Commonwealth Games Federation (2014), *Glasgow 2014 XX Commonwealth Games Post-Games Report*, available at: https://www.thecgf.com/games/2014/G2014-Official-Post-Games-Report.pdf

Commonwealth Secretariat and UNCTAD (n.d.), *Policy Guide on Youth Entrepreneurship*, available at: http://thecommonwealth.org/sites/default/files/press-release/documents/policyguideonyouthentrepreneurship.pdf

Cornelissen, S. (2009), 'A delicate balance: Major sport events and development', in Levermore, R. and A. Beacom (Eds), *Sport and International Development*, Palgrave Macmillan, Basingstoke, 76–97.

Cottle, E. and M. Rombaldi (2014), *Lessons from South Africa's FIFA World Cup, Brazil and its Legacy for Labour*, available at: http://www.global-labour-university.org/fileadmin/Summer_School_2014/EddieCottleCETIMbook2013FINAL.pdf

Crabbe, T. (2013), *Sportworks. Investing in Sport for Development and Creating the Business Case to Help Change the Lives of Disadvantaged Young People in the UK*, available at: http://www.substance.net/wp-content/uploads/2015/01/Sportworks-Full-Report.pdf

Darby, P. (2012), 'Gains versus drains: football academies and the export of highly skilled football labor', *Brown Journal of World Affairs*, Vol. 18, 265–277.

Darby, P. (2013), 'Moving players, traversing perspectives: Global value chains, production networks and Ghanaian football labour migration', *Geoforum*, Vol. 50, 43–53.

Darby, P., G. Akindes and M. Kirwin (2007), 'Football academies and the migration of African football labor to Europe', *Journal of Sport and Social Issues*, Vol. 31, 143–161.

Davies, L. E. (2010), 'Sport and economic regeneration: a winning combination?' *Sport in Society*, Vol. 13, 1438–1457.

Ernst and Young (2014), *Economic Impact 2022 Commonwealth Games South Africa: Durban Host City*, Ernst and Young Global Limited, available at: http://durban-2022.com/assets/files/Commonwealthgames.pdf

Fujiwara, D., L. Kudrna and P. Dolan (2014), *Quantifying the Social Impacts of Culture and Sport*, available at: https://www.gov.uk/government/uploads/system/uploads/attachment_data/file/304896/Quantifying_the_Social_Impacts_of_Culture_and_Sport.pdf

Gibson, H. J., K. Kaplanidou and S. J. Kang (2012), 'Small-scale event sport tourism: A case study in sustainable tourism', *Sport Management Review*, Vol. 15, 160–170.

Giulianotti, R. (2011), 'The sport, development and peace sector: a model of four social policy domains', *Journal of Social Policy*, 40(4), 757–776.

Gratton, C., G. Ramchandani, D. Wilson and D. Liu (2012), *The Global Economics of Sport*, Routledge, Abingdon.

Hayhurst, L. M. (2014), 'The "Girl Effect" and martial arts: social entrepreneurship and sport, gender and development in Uganda', *Gender, Place & Culture*, Vol. 21, 297–315.

Hinch, T. and J. Higham (2008), 'Sport tourism: a framework for research', in Weed, M. (Ed.), *Sport and Tourism: A Reader*, Routledge, Abingdon, 40–56.

International Labour Organization (ILO) (2013), *Global Employment Trends for Youth 2013: A Generation at Risk*, available at: http://www.ilo.org/global/research/global-reports/youth/2013/WCMS_212423/lang--en/index.htm

Kasamati, E. (2008), 'Economic aspects and the Summer Olympics: A review of related research', in Weed, M. (Ed.), *Sport and Tourism: A Reader*, Routledge, Abingdon, 314–327.

Kearney, A. T. (2014), *Winning in the Business of Sport*, available at: www.atkearney.com/documents/10192/5258876/Winning+in+the+Business+of+Sports.pdf/ed85b644-7633-469d-8f7a-99e4a50aadc8

Primault, D. (2006), 'Employment in sport', in Andreff, W. and S. Szymanski (Eds), *Handbook of the Economics of Sport*, Edward Elgar, Cheltenham.

Ratten, V. (2011), 'Sport-based entrepreneurship: towards a new theory of entrepreneurship and sport management', *International Entrepreneurship and Management Journal*, Vol. 7, 57–69.

Ratten, V. (2014), 'Collaborative entrepreneurship and the fostering of entrepreneurialism in developing countries', *International Journal of Social Entrepreneurship and Innovation*, Vol. 3, 137–149.

Sierra Leone Ministry of Sport (2015), *National Sports Policy of Sierra Leone*, Government of the Republic of Sierra Leone, Free Town.

Taks, M. (2016), 'The rise and fall of mega sport events: The future is non-mega sport events', in Auweele, Y. V., E. Cook and J. Parry (Eds), *Ethics and Governance in Sport: The Future of Sport Imagined*, Routledge, Abingdon, 84–93.

Thibault, L. (2009), 'Globalization of sport: an inconvenient truth', *Journal of Sport Management*, Vol. 23, 1–20.

UNESCO (2013), *Creative Economy Report: Widening Local Development Pathways*, available at: http://www.unesco.org/culture/pdf/creative-economy-report-2013.pdf

United Nations (2015), *The Millennium Development Goals Report 2015*, available at: http://www.un.org/millenniumgoals/2015_MDG_Report/pdf/MDG%202015%20rev%20(July%201).pdf

World Economic Forum (2009), *The Global Agenda 2009*, available at: www.weforum.org/pdf/globalagenda.pdf

Implementing a National Sport for Development and Peace Strategy

Sierra Leone

Mr Michael Mustapha
Deputy Director
Ministry of Sports
Government of Sierra Leone

The Sierra Leone Ministry of Sports published a new national sports policy in early 2015. One of the primary objectives of this policy is 'to provide for the use of sports as a cost effective means for development and peace initiatives' (Sierra Leone Ministry of Sport 2015).

To advance this objective, the Ministry of Sports has developed a National Sport for Development and Peace (SDP) Strategy and Action Plan. These documents articulate how sport will contribute towards the country's national development goals, including those related to peace-building and community cohesion (including Ebola recovery); health; education; equality and inclusion; and youth unemployment. Improving co-ordination and collaboration among ministries, departments and statutory agencies is a feature of the strategy. Together, the strategy and plan respond to SDG targets 17.14 and 17.15, which highlight the importance of nationally led and enhanced policy coherence for sustainable development.

Implementation is now underway, with a number of early successes. SDP initiatives are beginning to impact on people's lives and contribute to building stronger communities in Sierra Leone.

The successful hosting of the National Sport Jamboree, which included education and messaging on Ebola recovery, has increased confidence, improved social interaction and reduced stigma towards Ebola survivors. These efforts are positioned to contribute to SDG target 3.3, which is focused on combating communicable disease. In addition, basketball programmes aimed at promoting interaction among Sierra Leone youth have helped ease tensions and promote mutual respect between those loyal to different political parties. This work is contributing to SDG target 16.1, aimed at significantly reducing all forms of violence.

Meanwhile, in support of SDG target 4.7, focused on promoting a culture of peace and non-violence in education institutions, sports-based programmes are part of an overall strategy to address violence in academic institutions and reduce dropout, and through this increase skilled labour and literacy rates.

A linked initiative, the National Sport for All Commission, is tasked with promoting the ability of sport to contribute to the country's health objectives, including those linked to SDG target 3.4 related to reducing premature mortality from non-communicable disease. Citizens are encouraged to keep active and healthy through the Play for Life programme, which also aims to help keep some of Sierra Leone's traditional sports alive and pass them on to future generations.

(Continued)

Implementing a National Sport for Development and Peace Strategy (*cont.*)

Successes have been achieved as a result of strong governmental will and co-operation. The establishment of a National Steering Committee to oversee SDP activities has helped bridge the gap between the Ministry of Sports and other government agencies, and has led to more effective collaboration. Funding has been introduced, specifically for inter-community events that will promote social coexistence. Finally, the programme ensures that programme delivery occurs at accessible facilities.

If the objectives of the National Sports Policy are to be met, more facilities will need to be provided to encourage people to participate in physical exercise. Limited financing of course also remains a challenge, although early successes have led other public and private entities to express an interest in providing funds and upgrading sport facilities in communities.

SDP initiatives are beginning to improve lives and build stronger communities in Sierra Leone. The Ministry of Sports encourages other countries to explore its approach for their own use, and will share more SDP success stories with the international community in the future.

Chapter 10
Make Cities and Human Settlements Inclusive, Safe, Resilient and Sustainable (SDG 11)

10.1 Introduction

The *2030 Agenda for Sustainable Development* recognises that 'sustainable urban development and management are crucial to the quality of life of our people' (UNGA 2015, para. 34, 9). The concomitant adoption of SDG 11 represents an important extension of the MDGs, which did not give specific attention to global trends of increasing urbanisation. Fifty per cent of the global population currently live in cities (United Nations Sustainable Development Solutions Network [n.d.]), and urbanisation is expected to continue over the timeframe of the SDGs. Demographic and geographical changes mean that, by 2030, it is estimated that as many as 60 per cent of all urban dwellers will be under the age of 18 (UN-Habitat [n.d.]).

The 2030 Agenda for Sustainable Development recognises that 'sustainable urban development and management are crucial to the quality of life of our people'.

SDG 11 therefore represents recognition of the need to adopt a systematic approach that addresses infrastructure implications of population-level changes, in order to realise the full scope of the *2030 Agenda for Sustainable Development*. For example, there is strong and increasing evidence of the impact of the physical urban environment, and the provision of green space, on various aspects of health and well-being, and on patterns of health inequalities (Smit *et al.* 2011). UN-Habitat guidance indicates that a minimum of 15 per cent of an urban area should be allocated for open and green spaces and public facilities (United Nations Conference on Housing and Sustainable Urban Development 2015), which, in many cases, could include those for sport and active recreation. The benefit of such spaces 'where residents can gather [is that they] will promote social connectivity and diversity, thus making neighbourhoods more cohesive, lively, and ultimately more attractive to residents and investors alike'.

UN-Habitat guidance indicates that a minimum of 15 per cent of an urban area should be allocated for open and green spaces and public facilities.

It is therefore clear that SDG 11 and its specific targets have particular relevance to sport, and significant implications

Box 10.1 Enhancing the contribution of sport to Sustainable Development Goal 11: Key policy implications

- The provision of appropriate spaces and facilities for sport and active recreation can have wide-reaching and long-term impacts on participation, with resultant contributions across other development goals.
- Spaces and facilities for sport and active recreation should be designed to offer safety and accessibility for all.
- Multiple benefits can be drawn from integrating spaces for sport and active recreation into facilities for health, education and other services.
- Environmental principles and considerations of sustainable and community usage should inform the design of all spaces and facilities for sport, especially large-scale sport stadiums.
- Policies should encourage widespread involvement in the planning, design and management of spaces and facilities for sport and active recreation across the full range of national-level stakeholders and potential users.

SDG target 11.7 identifies the importance of designing and maintaining all spaces, including those suitable for sport and active recreation, in a way that provides safe and inclusive access for all in society.

for its contribution to other goals considered in this guide (see Box 10.1). SDG target 11.7 identifies the importance of designing and maintaining all spaces, including those suitable for sport and active recreation, in a way that provides safe and inclusive access for all in society. Planning and management of such spaces must be participatory, integrated and sustainable. SDG target 11.3, therefore, indicates both the importance and potential contribution of adopting such approaches within sport.

10.2 Analysis of sport and specific SDG targets

Target 11.7 By 2030, provide universal access to safe, inclusive and accessible, green and public spaces, in particular for women and children, older persons and persons with disabilities.

Policies that ensure that physical environments are conducive to participation can have long-term and population-level impacts.

The availability of spaces and facilities that are accessible, both by their proximity and design, is vital for participation and inclusion in sport and other forms of active recreation (Nicholson *et al.* 2010), which, in turn, is fundamental to contributions across the range of SDGs. For example, overall effects of urban planning and design on levels of physical activity and a range of related health outcomes are now well evidenced, especially in developed countries (Smit *et al.* 2011). Therefore, policies that ensure that physical environments are conducive to participation can have long-term and population-level impacts, extending what may be achieved by sport-based programming (Kaczynski and Henderson 2007). Such policies may be especially important in low- and medium-income countries where rapid urbanisation and related developments have resulted in the loss of outdoor spaces conducive to sport and active recreation (Akindes and Kirwan 2009).

Further work is required to enhance the evidence regarding the benefit of particular types of spaces or facilities for sport and active recreation (Kural 2010). However, spaces that allow both structured and unstructured engagement in sport and active recreation, alongside other leisure pursuits, can encourage wider family and community engagement, and more sustained use (McCormack *et al.* 2010). Furthermore, the integration of spaces for sport participation with facilities for health, education and other services can enable innovative approaches to collaborative provision, which have been recognised as important across multiple SDGs. In addition, such approaches may help to enhance community cohesion and foster greater engagement among user groups. In respect of schools in particular, there is recognition of both the challenges and significant possibilities of designing multi-purpose spaces that can be suitable for physical education, enable young people to engage in informal and inclusive activity outside of the curriculum and, where feasible, be available for use by the wider community (Fahlén 2011).

There is also growing recognition that integrated approaches to urban design and planning can promote access and enable physical activity to be built into daily routines (Heath *et al.* 2012). For example, there has been much interest in ensuring that urban infrastructure offers safe and accessible opportunities for walking and cycling, both to increase physical activity and reduce air pollution caused by other forms of transport (McCormack and Shiell 2011). Integrating messaging into the fabric of key community sites and into specific infrastructure – such as stairs, for example – to prompt immediate choices towards physical activity has also proved effective (Heath *et al.* 2012). Sporting facilities and spaces have also often been adorned with messages designed to educate participants and spectators about key health and social issues.

Integrated approaches to urban design and planning can promote access and enable physical activity to be built into daily routines.

Ongoing societal changes can give rise to opportunities and challenges with regard to providing appropriate spaces for sport-based activities. Patterns of participation in different types of sport vary considerably across and within different countries. Evidence from developed countries, especially, points to links between changing work–leisure patterns and increasing interest and participation in individualised and non-competitive forms of sport and active recreation (Kural 2010). As a result, innovative utilisation or re-orientation of existing outdoor community spaces for non-traditional forms of sport can be a feasible option in high-density urban environments (Kural 2010). For example, emergent evidence suggests that the allocation of small 'pocket parks', which allow safe participation in activities such as dance and informal exercise in urban areas, can be cost effective for promoting physical activity (Cohen *et al.* 2014).

Inclusion, accessibility and safety for all groups in society need to be key considerations in the design of all spaces and facilities.

Inclusion, accessibility and safety for all groups in society need to be key considerations in the design of all spaces and facilities. When close consideration is given to the needs of specific groups, this can result in improved and inclusive access for all (English Federation of Disability Sport 2013). For example, key barriers to participation by people with a disability can be overcome through suitably designed spaces and facilities which are appropriately equipped and provide appropriate external access (English Federation of Disability Sport 2013). These requirements link to more general design imperatives to ensure the availability of safe and accessible transport options, appropriate signage and information, secure lighting and visibility, and suitability for seasonal climate variations.

Linking to SDG 5, urban planners and sport policy-makers need to consider the particular needs of females, especially so in contexts in which dominant masculine cultures are deeply embedded. A balance needs to be struck to ensure that spaces and facilities are considered culturally acceptable for girls and women to participate in sport, while offering them appropriate levels of security and privacy (Brady 2005). Similarly, young people have emphasised the value they attach to spaces where they can gather in safety (Spaaij *et al.* 2014; UN-Habitat 2015), and it has been recognised that the provision of such spaces can act as a deterrent against community crime (Smit *et al.* 2011).

Beyond community-based spaces and facilities, the development and design of larger sport stadiums and venues, especially when connected to the hosting of sporting events, can have significant implications for the urban environments in which they are situated. Well-designed stadiums can become focal points in cities, readily identifiable by both residents and external stakeholders (Ahlfeldt and Maennig 2010). The potential environmental impacts of stadiums have also been increasingly recognised, and have become central to selection criteria for the hosting of sporting events (Cornelissen 2009). There are now numerous examples of stadiums that have been designed and constructed in line with environmental principles regarding material sourcing and use, energy conservation, and waste and water management (McCullough *et al.* 2015).

Well-designed stadiums can become focal points in cities, readily identifiable by both residents and external stakeholders.

Linking with SDG 3, there is emerging interest across some developed countries in the contribution that stadium design and management can make to health promotion among users (Drygas *et al.* 2013). Ensuring sustainable usage of stadiums, in part through community-oriented design and programming, is now regarded as a priority in respect of stadiums constructed for specific events. More broadly, as considered in the following section, policy-makers need to give consideration to the integration of stadium development and design into various national and municipal policy agendas, including those related to urban regeneration.

Target 11.3 By 2030, enhance inclusive and sustainable urbanisation and capacity for participatory, integrated and sustainable human settlement planning and management in all countries.

Enhancing urban environments and realising the benefits of spaces and facilities that are appropriate for sport requires well-considered planning and management from the national to community level. The importance of infrastructure for progress towards a variety of SDGs emphasises that the contributions of stakeholders from various sectors need to be aligned and, in some cases, reconciled. Conversely, dislocation between planning processes that influence the location, design, funding, management and programming in sporting spaces and facilities can result in significant under-utilisation and undermine their potential contribution across a variety of development goals (Fahlén 2011).

Enhancing urban environments and realising the benefits of spaces and facilities that are appropriate for sport requires well-considered planning and management from the national to community level.

Although national policy-makers and stakeholders may not have immediate responsibility for planning in particular urban areas, the policy instruments available to them can help to ensure appropriate provision of suitable spaces and facilities. National-level data and analysis on the geographical distribution of particular types of spaces and facilities, both for participation and high-performance sport, can support effective planning by all stakeholders through identifying priority areas where new or additional developments may be located (Paramio-Salcines 2014). National policies and the regulatory frameworks enforcing them can also ensure the preservation of spaces that may be utilised for sport and active recreation in urban areas (see Figure 10.1). Utilisation of expertise within sport federations can also contribute to specifying quality design criteria for different types of spaces and facilities.

Figure 10.1 Making safe, accessible spaces for sport and physical activity available to all

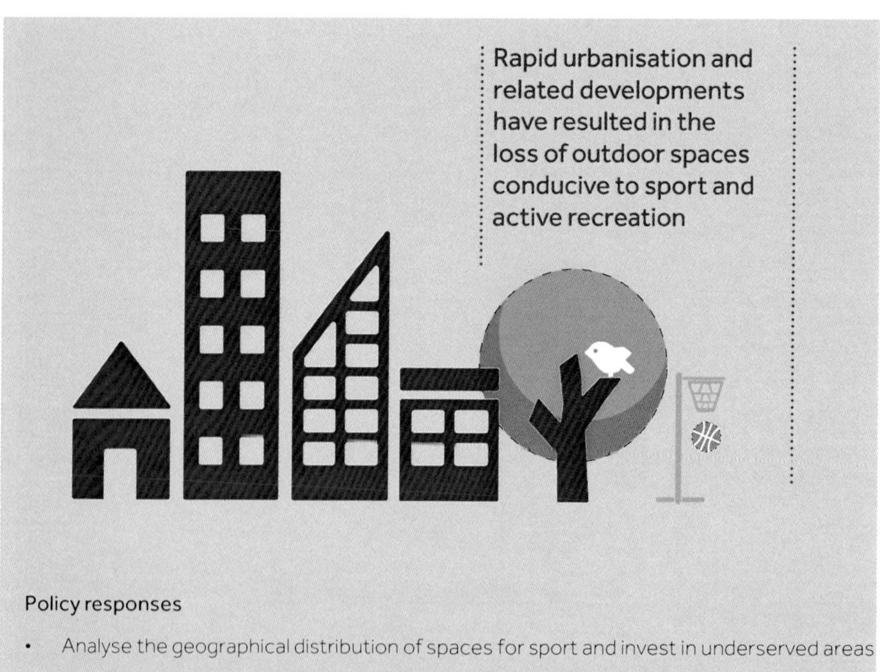

Policy responses

- Analyse the geographical distribution of spaces for sport and invest in underserved areas
- Integrate new spaces for sport participation with facilities for health, education and other services
- Make school sport facilities available for wider community use after hours
- Provide design guidance for spaces and facilities for sport
- Prioritise accessibility for people with a disability
- Ensure spaces are culturally acceptable for girls and women with appropriate levels of security and privacy
- Create 'pocket parks' for safe participation in activities such as dance and informal exercise

Source: Akindes and Kirwan (2009); Brady (2005); Cohen *et al.* (2014); Heath *et al.* (2012); Paramio-Salcines (2014)

Roles in providing, securing and directing investment in infrastructure and urban environments may span national, sub-national and local levels. Although some responsibilities for public spending can be devolved, national funding initiatives can prioritise the integration of provisions for sport and active recreation into infrastructure projects in other sectors, such as education, health and transport. As addressed under SDG 4, for example, national guidelines and requirements can ensure that school facilities include appropriate specifications for physical education and sport. National analysis can also enable inward investment in sport facilities to be best directed to address national and local development needs and goals.

National funding may contribute to the development of community-based sporting facilities and spaces, but overall responsibility for this type of provision most commonly resides with sub-national and local government. Return on investment, which may encompass wider benefits of improved community well-being and safety, can be particularly evident in respect of local developments. As such, it is at the local level that public–private partnerships to generate investment in sporting facilities and spaces may be realised.

At the levels of sub-national and local government, there are different models through which the development of sporting infrastructure can be integrated with, and contribute to, overall urban planning goals (Davies 2010). In a 'sports-led regeneration' model, event hosting and/or the construction of sport stadiums represent catalysts for broader urban planning and development projects. The high-profile nature of sport-led regeneration can stimulate collective action and bring forward timescales for infrastructure developments that are of benefit beyond the specific sport stadium or event (Smith 2012).

An alternative 'sport regeneration' model is centred on cross-sector, area-based strategies for urban development which integrate planning for sporting spaces and facilities from the outset. Sporting events and stadiums can be associated with this model, but it also provides greater scope for the integrated development of a range of spaces and facilities identified earlier in the chapter as offering potential to increase sport participation and address other SDGs. In practice, the connection between urban planning and the development of sporting infrastructure has often been more ad hoc than could be achieved by the adoption of either of the suggested models

(Davies 2010). The planned instigation of a Commonwealth Sports Cities Network (Commonwealth Games Federation 2015) may offer encouragement towards more strategic approaches to integrated infrastructure development by contributing to sharing cross-country and cross-municipality learning.

The processes of urban planning and management can benefit from engaging the full spectrum of stakeholders and population groups that are involved in or are affected by developments.

The processes of urban planning and management can benefit from engaging the full spectrum of stakeholders and population groups that are involved in or are affected by developments (AlQahtany *et al.* 2013). Public consultations can demonstrate and garner support for the development of sporting spaces and facilities. Participatory and inclusive approaches to community engagement can be especially valuable, as urban planning processes are often the preserve of adult males (UN-Habitat 2015). Gaining input into the design of spaces and facilities from young people of both genders may be challenging, but it can result in creative innovations and greater ownership and use, and reduce any likelihood of subsequent vandalism (CABE Space and CABE Education 2004; UN-Habitat 2012). Beyond design issues, sport and development organisations are often well placed to contribute to community-based management and use of spaces and facilities. The value of doing so can also be enhanced through specific sport-based approaches that have been used to educate and enlist participants in the maintenance and improvement of environmental conditions in their own communities (Coalter 2010).

10.3 The means of implementation: Policy options for Sustainable Development Goal 11

Contributions towards funding for spaces and facilities can be drawn from national and local governments, and can also be levered through partnerships with private and civil society organisations.

Policy development and effective implementation that provides valuable, accessible, safe and inclusive spaces and facilities for sport and active recreation require the involvement of a range of stakeholders at national, local and community levels. National-level policy-makers can guide, regulate and monitor the planning and design of all spaces, including those that can be used for sport and active recreation. Contributions towards funding for spaces and facilities can be drawn from national and local governments, and can also be levered through partnerships with private and civil society organisations. The engagement of local stakeholders and potential users allows valuable contributions to the effective design and management of spaces and facilities, and their ongoing usage.

Table 10.1 Policy options to enhance the contribution of sport to SDG 11

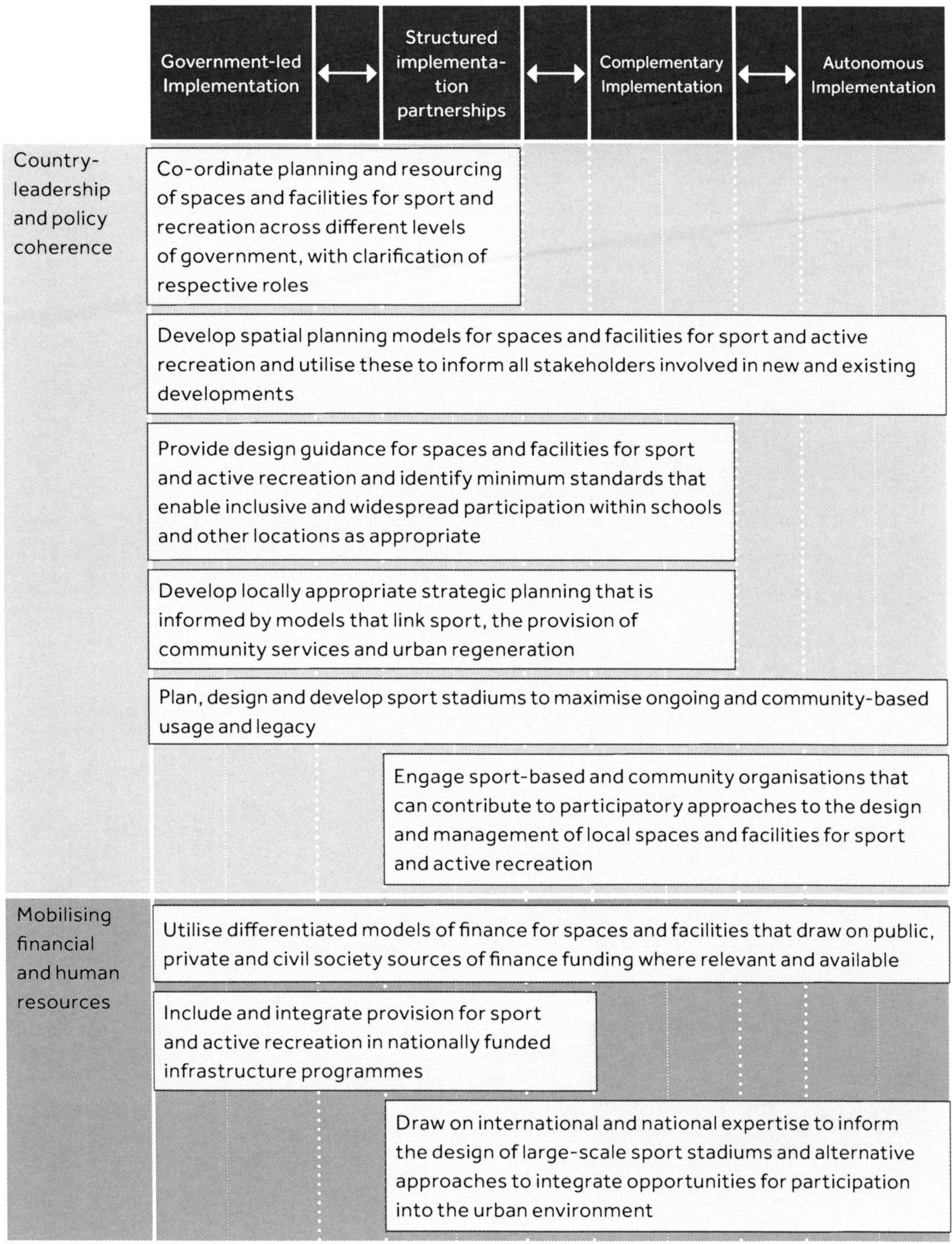

<table>
<tr><th></th><th>Government-led Implementation</th><th>Structured implementation partnerships</th><th>Complementary Implementation</th><th>Autonomous Implementation</th></tr>
<tr><td rowspan="6">Country-leadership and policy coherence</td><td colspan="2">Co-ordinate planning and resourcing of spaces and facilities for sport and recreation across different levels of government, with clarification of respective roles</td><td></td><td></td></tr>
<tr><td colspan="4">Develop spatial planning models for spaces and facilities for sport and active recreation and utilise these to inform all stakeholders involved in new and existing developments</td></tr>
<tr><td colspan="3">Provide design guidance for spaces and facilities for sport and active recreation and identify minimum standards that enable inclusive and widespread participation within schools and other locations as appropriate</td><td></td></tr>
<tr><td colspan="3">Develop locally appropriate strategic planning that is informed by models that link sport, the provision of community services and urban regeneration</td><td></td></tr>
<tr><td colspan="4">Plan, design and develop sport stadiums to maximise ongoing and community-based usage and legacy</td></tr>
<tr><td></td><td colspan="3">Engage sport-based and community organisations that can contribute to participatory approaches to the design and management of local spaces and facilities for sport and active recreation</td></tr>
<tr><td rowspan="3">Mobilising financial and human resources</td><td colspan="4">Utilise differentiated models of finance for spaces and facilities that draw on public, private and civil society sources of finance funding where relevant and available</td></tr>
<tr><td colspan="2">Include and integrate provision for sport and active recreation in nationally funded infrastructure programmes</td><td></td><td></td></tr>
<tr><td></td><td colspan="3">Draw on international and national expertise to inform the design of large-scale sport stadiums and alternative approaches to integrate opportunities for participation into the urban environment</td></tr>
</table>

(Continued)

Table 10.1 Policy options to enhance the contribution of sport to SDG 11 (*cont.*)

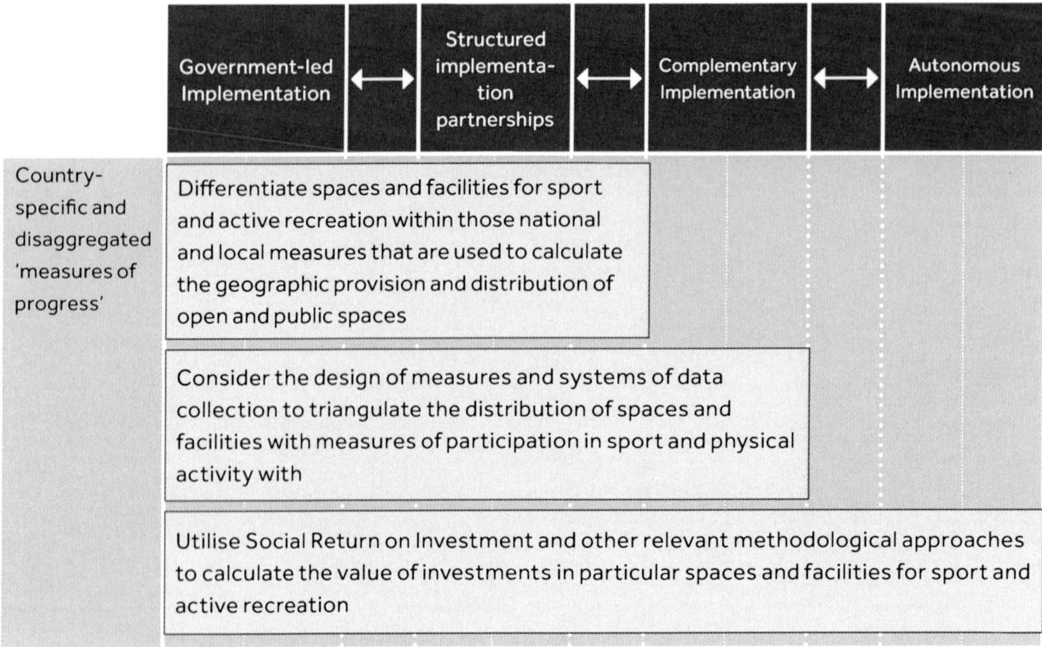

	Government-led Implementation	⟷	Structured implementa-tion partnerships	⟷	Complementary Implementation	⟷	Autonomous Implementation
Country-specific and disaggregated 'measures of progress'	Differentiate spaces and facilities for sport and active recreation within those national and local measures that are used to calculate the geographic provision and distribution of open and public spaces						
	Consider the design of measures and systems of data collection to triangulate the distribution of spaces and facilities with measures of participation in sport and physical activity with						
	Utilise Social Return on Investment and other relevant methodological approaches to calculate the value of investments in particular spaces and facilities for sport and active recreation						

References

Ahlfeldt, G. and W. Maennig (2010), 'Stadium architecture and urban development from the perspective of urban economics', *International Journal of Urban and Regional Research*, Vol. 34, 629–646.

Akindes, G. and M. Kirwan (2009), 'Sport as international aid: Assisting development or promoting under-development in Sub-Saharan Africa?', in Levermore, R. and A. Beacom (Eds), *Sport and International Development*, Macmillan, Basingtoke, 215–245.

AlQahtany, A., Y. Rezgui and H. Li (2013), 'A proposed model for sustainable urban planning development for environmentally friendly communities', *Architectural Engineering and Design Management*, Vol. 9, 176–194.

Brady, M. (2005), 'Creating safe spaces and building social assets for young women in the developing world: A new role for sports', *Women's Studies Quarterly*, Vol. 33, 35–49.

CABE Space and CABE Education (2004), *What Would You Do With this Space? Involving Young People in the Design and Care of Urban Spaces*, available at: http://webarchive.nationalarchives.gov.uk/20110118095356/http://www.cabe.org.uk/publications/what-would-you-do-with-this-space

Coalter, F. (2010), 'The politics of sport-for-development: Limited focus programmes and broad gauge problems?' *International Review for the Sociology of Sport*, Vol. 45, 295–314.

Cohen, D. A., T. Marsh, S. Williamson, B. Han, K. P. Derose, D. Golinelli and T. L. McKenzie (2014), 'The potential for pocket parks to increase physical activity', *American Journal of Health Promotion*, Vol. 28, S19–S26.

Commonwealth Games Federation (2015), *Transformation 2022: The Commonwealth Games Federation Strategic Plan 2015–2022*, available at: http://thecgf.com/

Cornelissen, S. (2009), 'A delicate balance: Major sport events and development', in Levermore, R. and A. Beacom (Eds), *Sport and International Development*, Palgrave Macmillan, Basingstoke, 76–97.

Davies, L. E. (2010), 'Sport and economic regeneration: a winning combination?' *Sport in Society*, Vol. 13, 1438–1457.

Drygas, W., J. Ruszkowska, M. Philpott, O. Björkström, M. Parker, R. Ireland, F. Roncarolo and M. Tenconi (2013), 'Good practices and health policy analysis in European sports stadia: results from the "Healthy Stadia" project', *Health Promotion International*, Vol. 28, 157–165.

English Federation of Disability Sport (2013), *Access for All: Opening Doors*, available at: http://www.efds.co.uk/assets/0001/6752/Access_for_all_November_2015.pdf

Fahlén, J. (2011), 'Urgent expectations and silenced knowledge: On spontaneous sport space as public health promoter and sport stimulator', *European Journal for Sport and Society*, Vol. 8, 167–191.

Heath, G. W., D. C. Parra, O. L. Sarmiento, L. B. Andersen, N. Owen, S. Goenka, F. Montes and R. C. Brownson (2012), 'Evidence-based intervention in physical activity: lessons from around the world', *The Lancet*, Vol. 380, 272–281.

Kaczynski, A. T. and K. A. Henderson (2007), 'Environmental correlates of physical activity: a review of evidence about parks and recreation', *Leisure Sciences*, Vol. 29, 315–354.

Kural, R (2010), 'Changing spaces for sports', *Sport in Society*, Vol. 13, 300–313.

McCormack, G. R., M. Rock, A. M. Toohey and D. Hignell (2010), 'Characteristics of urban parks associated with park use and physical activity: a review of qualitative research', *Health and Place*, Vol. 16, 712–726.

McCormack, G. R. and A. Shiell (2011), 'In search of causality: a systematic review of the relationship between the built environment and physical activity among adults', *International Journal of Behavioral Nutrition and Physical Activity*, Vol. 8, 2–11.

McCullough, B. P., M. E. Pfahl and S. Nguyen (2015), 'The green waves of environmental sustainability in sport', *Sport in Society*, available at: http://www.tandfonline.com/doi/abs/10.1080/17430437.2015.1096251

Nicholson, M., R. Hoye and B. Houlihan (Eds) (2010), *Participation in Sport: International Policy Perspectives*, Routledge, Abingdon.

Paramio-Salcines, J. L. (2014), 'Sport and urban regeneration', in Henry, I. and L. M. Ko (Eds), *Handbook of Sport Policy*, Routledge, Abingdon.

Smit, W., T. Hancock, J. Kumaresen, C. Santos-Burgoa, R. Sánchez-Kobashi Meneses and S. Friel (2011), 'Toward a research and action agenda on urban planning/design and health equity in cities in low and middle-income countries', *Journal of Urban Health*, Vol. 88, 875–885.

Smith, A. (2012), *Events and Urban Regeneration: The Strategic Use of Events to Revitalise Cities*, Routledge, Abingdon.

Spaaij, R., J. Magee and R. Jeanes (2014), *Sport and Social Exclusion in Global Society*, Routledge, Abingdon.

UN General Assembly (UNGA) (2015), *Transforming our World: The 2030 Agenda for Sustainable Development*, available at: www.un.org/ga/search/view_doc.asp?symbol=A/70/L.1andLang=E

UN-Habitat (2012), *Young People, Participation and Sustainable Development in an Urbanizing World*, available at: http://unhabitat.org/books/young-people-participation-and-sustainable-development-in-an-urbanizing-world/#

UN-Habitat (2015), *Youth and their needs with public space*, available at: https://issuu.com/unhabitatyouthunit/docs/youth_-_public_space_and_needs___lo

UN-Habitat (n.d.), *Youth*, available at: http://unhabitat.org/urban-themes/youth/

United Nations Conference on Housing and Sustainable Urban Development (2015), *Habitat III Issue Papers: 11 Public Space*, available at: http://unhabitat.org/wp-content/uploads/2015/04/Habitat-III-Issue-Paper-11_Public-Space-2.0.compressed.pdf

United Nations Sustainable Development Solutions Network (n.d.), *Campaign for an Urban Development Goal, #urban SDG*, available at: http://urbansdg.org/

Chapter 11
Promote Peaceful and Inclusive Societies for Sustainable Development, Provide Access to Justice for All, and Build Effective, Accountable and Inclusive Institutions at All Levels (SDG 16)

11.1 Introduction

The integrated and universal approach that is fundamental to the *2030 Agenda for Sustainable Development* is well represented in SDG 16. This goal represents a specific and important extension to the preceding MDGs and is based on the recognition that:

> *Sustainable development cannot be realized without peace and security; and peace and security will be at risk without sustainable development.*
>
> (UNGA 2015, para. 7, 3)

Equally, sustainable development, peace and security are dependent on universal access to justice and the effective implementation of good governance principles by institutions that are transparent and accountable. The *2030 Agenda for Sustainable Development* commits to uphold longstanding human rights principles that remain relevant and fundamental to emergent threats to peace and justice. As such, SDG 16 is strongly aligned with the respect for human rights, the values of tolerance, respect and understanding, and the principles of good governance expressed in the Commonwealth Charter (Commonwealth Secretariat 2013).

Sustainable development, peace and security are dependent on universal access to justice and the effective implementation of good governance principles by institutions that are transparent and accountable.

Similarly balanced considerations also apply with respect to the potential contribution of sport to SDG 16 (see Box 11.1). Longstanding and emergent examples of sport-based approaches that seek to prevent or alleviate various forms of violence can make contributions to SDG target 16.1. Addressing changes in the nature of global violence requires new and adapted strategies, and there may be potential for sport-based approaches to be implemented flexibly in response to these challenges.

The high and growing profile of corruption and doping in sport, and the manipulation of sporting competition serves to emphasise the importance of ensuring that sporting institutions prioritise the principles of good governance encompassed in SDG targets 16.5, 16.6 and 16.7.

However, there is also increasing recognition and concern regarding threats to the integrity of sport that can undermine the potential of sport to contribute positively to peace and inclusion, and to other goals. SDG target 16.2 draws attention to the need to strengthen efforts to combat abuse and all forms of violence against children. The high and growing profile of corruption and doping in sport, and the manipulation of sporting competition serves to emphasise the importance of ensuring that sporting institutions prioritise the principles of good governance encompassed in SDG targets 16.5, 16.6 and 16.7.

Existing and developing international impetus, conventions and guidance to address aspects of integrity in sport are relevant across these targets. Within the *Declaration of Berlin,* one of the three commissions that provide specific commitments and recommendations is dedicated to 'Preserving the Integrity of Sport' (UNESCO 2013). Furthermore, the publication of a Commonwealth consensus on integrity in sport follows a request made at the 6th Commonwealth Sports Ministers Meeting and continues work by the Commonwealth Advisory Board of Sport in these areas. This guide, and the policy options presented, draw on and are aligned with these broader international and Commonwealth commitments.

Box 11.1 Enhancing the contribution of sport to Sustainable Development Goal 16: Key policy implications

- Sport can be used as both a high-profile and participatory approach towards the reduction of violence and promotion of peace, but caution must be applied as regards the impact of these approaches in isolation.
- Increased recognition of abuse and violence against children is vital in order to improve the development and implementation of safeguarding policies.
- Protecting and preserving the integrity of sport in all forms and at all levels is recognised as vital, without which contributions to various SDGs would be undermined.
- Safeguarding children in sport and preserving the integrity of sport both require:
  - prioritisation and leadership across and by all sporting organisations
  - government agencies to take significant roles in promoting and ensuring the implementation of relevant policies.

11.2 Analysis of sport and specific SDG targets

Target 16.1 Significantly reduce all forms of violence and related death rates everywhere.

Violence may be perpetrated at and across international, state, intra-state and local community levels. The different timescales over which particular forms and occurrences of violence have been sustained is also a relevant consideration for this target, as are the needs of societies, groups and individuals that are emerging from violence and conflict. Sport may have degrees of relevance across all of these dimensions. However, given the deep-rooted and complex causes of violence and conflict, there must also be sensitivity and realism with regard to the potential contribution of sport-based interventions.

Given the deep-rooted and complex causes of violence and conflict, there must also be sensitivity and realism with regard to the potential contribution of sport-based interventions.

The high profile of sport athletes, teams and events gives them significant symbolic status with respect to the promotion of peace, inclusion and social cohesion. National teams and athletes can serve to cultivate collective identities within countries that have suffered from societal divisions (Sen 2011). Internationally, the United Nations' adoption of the Olympic Truce every two years draws on the status of the Summer and Winter Games to promote the values of peace (Burleson 2012). Similar aspirations underpin the vision of the Commonwealth Games Federation and also interventions by athletes who have, or may develop, an association with specific contexts that have been subject to conflict and violence (Wilson *et al.* 2015). Concerns that the impact of such interventions or events can be ephemeral must be addressed by connecting them to longer-term peace-building processes. The management of risk also needs to be prioritised, as high-profile sport events and competitions have previously been associated with violence, conflict and nationalism, and may also be a high-profile target for terrorism (Houlihan and Giulianotti 2012).

More participatory sport-based approaches within localities and communities can also make use of the popularity of sport and the flexible methods of delivery. In different contexts, sport has been used in a variety of ways towards different objectives associated with peace, violence reduction and inclusion. Community-based participation and volunteering in sport may enable the engagement of otherwise marginalised groups and allow the development of shared identities and social ties (Sen 2011). Specific interventions have used sport to help enable

Community-based participation and volunteering in sport may enable the engagement of otherwise marginalised groups and allow the development of shared identities and social ties.

a sense of normalcy among participants deeply and recently affected by conflict (Ha and Lyras 2013). More commonly, sport-based approaches have sought to contribute to crime reduction through both providing diversionary activities and, more importantly, offering opportunities that enable personal and social development which may, for some, form part of rehabilitation programmes (Nichols 2010). Whereas widespread participation may be encouraged in sport-based approaches designed to contribute to peace and inclusion, those seeking to reduce engagement in crime may benefit from a more intensive approach, working with more restricted numbers of young people identified through their involvement, or risk of involvement, in crime (Coalter 2013).

Sport can be perceived as a neutral space, but this value must be reflected in the specific design of activities which must offer opportunities for the sharing of experiences and cohesion.

Externally initiated interventions must consider how to appropriately build local capacity and structures to support the long-term development required in areas affected by violence, crime and conflict.

As with the sport-based approaches considered in respect of SDGs 4 and 5, the environment within which engagement and participation occurs is vital. Sport can be perceived as a neutral space, but this value must be reflected in the specific design of activities which must offer opportunities for the sharing of experiences and cohesion. Care must be taken when implementing traditional forms of competition, as this can potentially reinforce division. The status and skills of those leading activities are also an important consideration for various sport-based approaches to peace, inclusion, crime and rehabilitation. For peace-building and violence reduction, for example, leaders who are not personally associated with conflict may be seen as impartial but, equally, they must have a deep understanding of local contexts and guard against any perceptions of cultural imperialism (Sugden 2010). Similarly, externally initiated interventions must consider how to appropriately build local capacity and structures to support the long-term development required in areas affected by violence, crime and conflict (Schulenkorf 2010). This reinforces the need for sport-based interventions to be integrated into complementary, multi-stakeholder approaches which may support scaling-up and foster broader impacts.

Target 16.2 End abuse, exploitation, trafficking and all forms of violence against and torture of children.

UNICEF reports that abuse and violence against children occur globally, across countries of all different types and across all cultural groups (UNICEF 2014). Sport can be a particular context for abuse and violence against children, although this is under-recognised by some stakeholders (Rhind *et al.* 2016).

Children participating in sport, especially girls, can be particularly vulnerable because of their potential reliance on the support of coaches and others in positions of influence (Lang and Hartill 2014). As recognised in relation to SDG 8, young people in some contexts may also be at risk of exploitation in sections of the sport industry, and this can especially be the case if others seek to profit by offering local and global pathways into professional sport careers. Without progress to end abuse, exploitation and violence against children in sport, the contribution of sport to address other SDGs, and especially those concerned with health, education and gender, will be undermined.

Without progress to end abuse, exploitation and violence against children in sport, the contribution of sport to address other SDGs, and especially those concerned with health, education and gender, will be undermined.

The key reference point for all efforts to end abuse and violence against children is the United Nations Convention on the Rights of the Child which requires states to undertake:

> *all appropriate legislative, administrative, social and educational measures to protect the child from all forms of physical or mental violence, injury or abuse, neglect or negligent treatment, maltreatment or exploitation.*
>
> (United Nations 1989)

More recently and specifically, the United Nations Office of Sport for Development and Peace (UNOSDP 2010), UNICEF (UNICEF 2010) and the Commonwealth (Commonwealth Secretariat 2016) have called for specific policies and structures to prevent and respond to abuse and violence against children in sport. The Commonwealth Secretariat, UNICEF and prominent civil society sport and development organisations have responded to these calls through forming the International Safeguarding Children in Sport Working Group, which has developed and promoted a set of safeguards (International Safeguarding Children in Sport Working Group 2014) intended to be relevant to all organisations in sport (see case study below).

The importance of safeguarding the welfare of all children in sport, rather than focusing more specifically on protecting those who are particularly vulnerable to abuse and violence, is becoming increasingly recognised. However, only a limited range of countries have policies in place for safeguarding children in sport and, equally, policy implementation poses significant problems in some contexts (Lang and Hartill 2014). Within different contexts and across various sport organisations, the cultural change required to address what is an urgent problem can be slow. There remains significant variation in the extent to which all organisations in sport, both within and across countries, have adopted child-centred pedagogies. Such pedagogies place specific focus on the rights of children, encourage their input into decision making and thereby support integration with strategies for protection and safeguarding (Twyford 2016).

All governments have a responsibility to contribute significantly to enabling the prevention of abuse and violence within sport.

Finally, gathering relevant evidence to prioritise action and improve protection and safeguarding practice is an underdeveloped requirement in many countries.

Irrespective of any concerns regarding the autonomy of sport (Lang and Hartill 2014), all governments have a responsibility to contribute significantly to enabling the prevention of abuse and violence within sport. Cross-sectoral government policies, procedures and systems for child protection and safeguarding can offer important points of reference and referral for sport organisations. Expertise that may exist within government ministries or civil society organisations with responsibility for, or roles specifically in relation to, children and young people can contribute to awareness raising and capacity-building where it is required within sport. The sharing of effective practices from different sectors can also contribute to cultural change within organisations and, in some contexts, it may be feasible for sport to contribute to leadership in this regard. Finally, gathering relevant evidence to prioritise action and improve protection and safeguarding practice is an underdeveloped requirement in many countries (Twyford 2016).

International safeguards for children in sport

International Safeguarding Children in Sport Founders Group

Sport can educate and empower children facing adversity. It can help children build essential life skills and better futures. Sport can improve health, fitness and educational quality, leading to improved academic achievement, school readiness and attendance. But sport can only do this if it is delivered in a safe and supportive environment.

Sport, as with other social domains, can bring risks of violence and abuse. Some risks to children are unique to sport, such as those of all forms of abuse to elite young athletes, training when injured and hazing. There is growing awareness among sport organisations, researchers and athlete advocates that violence and abuse in sport needs to be addressed across the sporting landscape, in all countries, irrespective of size or location.[1] Safeguarding is an attempt to mitigate this issue through taking actions to ensure everyone connected to sport is safe.

SDG target 16.1, on reducing all forms of violence, and SDG target 16.2, on ending all forms of violence against children, places an additional responsibility on all actors to work towards the elimination of violence against children in all spheres, including sport.

(Continued)

International safeguards for children in sport (*cont.*)

The International Safeguarding Children in Sport Founders Group, working with more than 50 organisations from a diverse range of countries and contexts, has developed international safeguards for children in sport. These set out the actions that all organisations working in sport should have in place to ensure that children are safe from harm.

They have been informed by research with a diverse range of organisations and incorporate perspectives from different countries and stakeholder groups. The eight safeguards are:

1. Developing Your Policy
2. Procedures for Managing Safeguarding Concerns
3. Advice and Support
4. Minimising Risks to Children
5. Guidelines for Behaviour
6. Recruiting, Training and Communicating
7. Working with Partners
8. Monitoring and Evaluating.

To support their implementation, practical guidance and resources have been produced for any organisation working with children in sport. Eight key pillars should underpin the development, adoption and implementation of the safeguards, summarised by the acronym CHILDREN.

Key pillars in the development, adoption and implementation of safeguards for children in sport

Pillar	Description
Cultural sensitivity	There is a clear need for flexibility within international safeguards such that they can be tailored to the cultural and social norms of the context
Holistic	Safeguarding should be viewed as integrated into all aspects of an organisation as opposed to being an additional element
Incentives	There needs to be a clear reason for individuals and an organisation to work towards the safeguards
Leadership	The safeguards need to have strong support from those working in key leadership roles
Dynamic	The safeguarding systems within an organisation need to be continually reviewed and adapted to maintain their relevance and effectiveness
Resources	The implementation of the safeguards needs to be supported by appropriate resources (e.g. human, time and financial)
Engaging stakeholders	A democratic approach should be adopted which invites and listens to the voices of those in and around the sport (e.g. parents, coaches, community leaders)
Networks	An organisation's progress towards the safeguards will be strengthened by developing networks with other organisations working towards the safeguards

(*Continued*)

International safeguards for children in sport (*cont.*)

The mounting evidence of the need to better safeguard children in sport, coupled with the global call to action within targets 16.1 and 16.2 of the SDGs, means that all stakeholders across the sporting landscape must work to ensure that sport is delivered in a safe and supportive environment for all. The international safeguards for children in sport provide a tool and resource to support this objective.

Access these international safeguards for children in sport at: http://www.brunel.ac.uk/environment/themes/welfare-health-wellbeing/research-projects/developing-the-international-safeguards-for-children-in-sport

Target 16.5 Substantially reduce corruption and bribery in all their forms.

Target 16.6 Develop effective, accountable and transparent institutions at all levels.

Target 16.7 Ensure responsive, inclusive, participatory and representative decision making at all levels.

Various forms of corruption and bribery present significant threats to the integrity of sport.

Various forms of corruption and bribery present significant threats to the integrity of sport. Problems of doping, the manipulation of sporting competitions, and financial misappropriation and fraud are by no means new but have become increasingly prominent within sport. Such problems may share links to the commercialised and globalised nature of modern sport, but equally can be evident across different levels in sport, across the range of individual roles and different types of institutions involved in sport, and across diverse country contexts.

The Declaration of Berlin centrally recognises that concerted efforts are required to uphold the core values of sport, and also to realise its social potential.

Global efforts to protect and enhance the integrity of sport have intensified. The *Declaration of Berlin* centrally recognises that concerted efforts are required to uphold the core values of sport, and also to realise its social potential (UNESCO 2013). Communiqués from Commonwealth Sports Ministers Meetings have reinforced the importance of work undertaken by the Commonwealth Advisory Body on Sport (CABOS) to preserve the integrity of sport (CABOS 2015). The contribution of specific global institutions, such as the World Anti-Doping Agency, have been complemented more recently by civil society advocacy and expertise provided by organisations such as the International Centre for Sport Security and Transparency International (Transparency International 2015).

Good governance in sport and its organisations is central to addressing all forms of corruption and bribery. Although structures and institutions differ across sports and from international to national and local levels (Chappelet and Mrkonjic 2013), there is increasing acceptance and harmonisation of principles for good governance in sport. Terminology can vary, but different statements of good governance in sport commonly recognise principles associated with democratic appointment and decision-making processes; accountability within and beyond the organisation; transparency in respect of financial and other matters; integrity and the adoption of codes of ethics; and solidarity across different levels and aspects of sport (IOC 2008; Commonwealth Secretariat 2016; Alm [n.d.]).

Good governance in sport and its organisations is central to addressing all forms of corruption and bribery.

While it is the case that international efforts and orientations have shaped the development of principles of good governance for sport, these are increasingly, but somewhat variably, being applied at national levels. National governments have a key role in monitoring and encouraging the implementation of good governance principles by sport federations and other sporting organisations within their jurisdiction. These responsibilities respond to the recognition that the longstanding autonomy of sport organisations is predicated on their compliance with relevant standards of good governance (UNESCO 2013). Increasingly, public funding for sporting organisations is made on the condition that they apply standards of good governance. National laws should also be enforced for all instances of corruption in sport, and international legal frameworks should also be applied in relevant cases and contexts, for example in respect of the UNESCO International Convention against Doping in Sport (UNESCO 2005).

National governments have a key role in monitoring and encouraging the implementation of good governance principles by sport federations and other sporting organisations within their jurisdiction.

Collective and co-operative efforts, across governmental and sporting stakeholders, are also vital for addressing threats to the integrity of sport. These efforts require sufficient financial resources and institutional and human capacity, and these can be increased through both in-country and international partnerships (Hanstad and Houlihan 2015). International co-operation and information sharing is also necessary, given that aspects of corruption, including doping, operate globally. Within individual countries, engagement among law enforcement agencies and sporting stakeholders can deny and curtail opportunities for corruption. The comprehensive provision of education to mitigate risks of engagement in corrupt practices by athletes, coaches and all other sporting stakeholders is a further development that is enhanced by drawing on the collective capacity across and beyond the sport movement.

11.3 The means of implementation: Policy options for Sustainable Development Goal 16

The use of sport-based approaches to contribute to peace and the reduction of violence has to be implemented carefully, drawing on in-depth understanding of local contexts.

The introduction to this chapter recognised the connections between the different aspects of SDG 16. However, the preceding analysis demonstrates that there is diversity in the ways in which sport-based approaches may contribute to different SDG 16 targets (see Figure 11.1). This diversity means that options for policy implementation are similarly varied and need to make use of different policy instruments. The use of sport-based approaches to contribute to peace and the reduction of violence has to be implemented carefully, drawing on in-depth understanding of local contexts. Governmental interventions to support or scale-up such sport-based approaches need similar sensitivity, especially in contexts in which civil society organisations may be best placed to lead initiatives. Well-judged approaches to policy implementation are also required to address threats to the integrity of sport, including abuse and violence against children and various forms of corruption. Policy-makers have to assess the appropriate balance between the use of different policy instruments – including regulation and enforcement, funding and financial incentives, and education and capacity-building – and these should be supported by effective collection and use of various forms of information.

Figure 11.1 Contributing to SDG 16 by building effective, accountable and inclusive sporting institutions

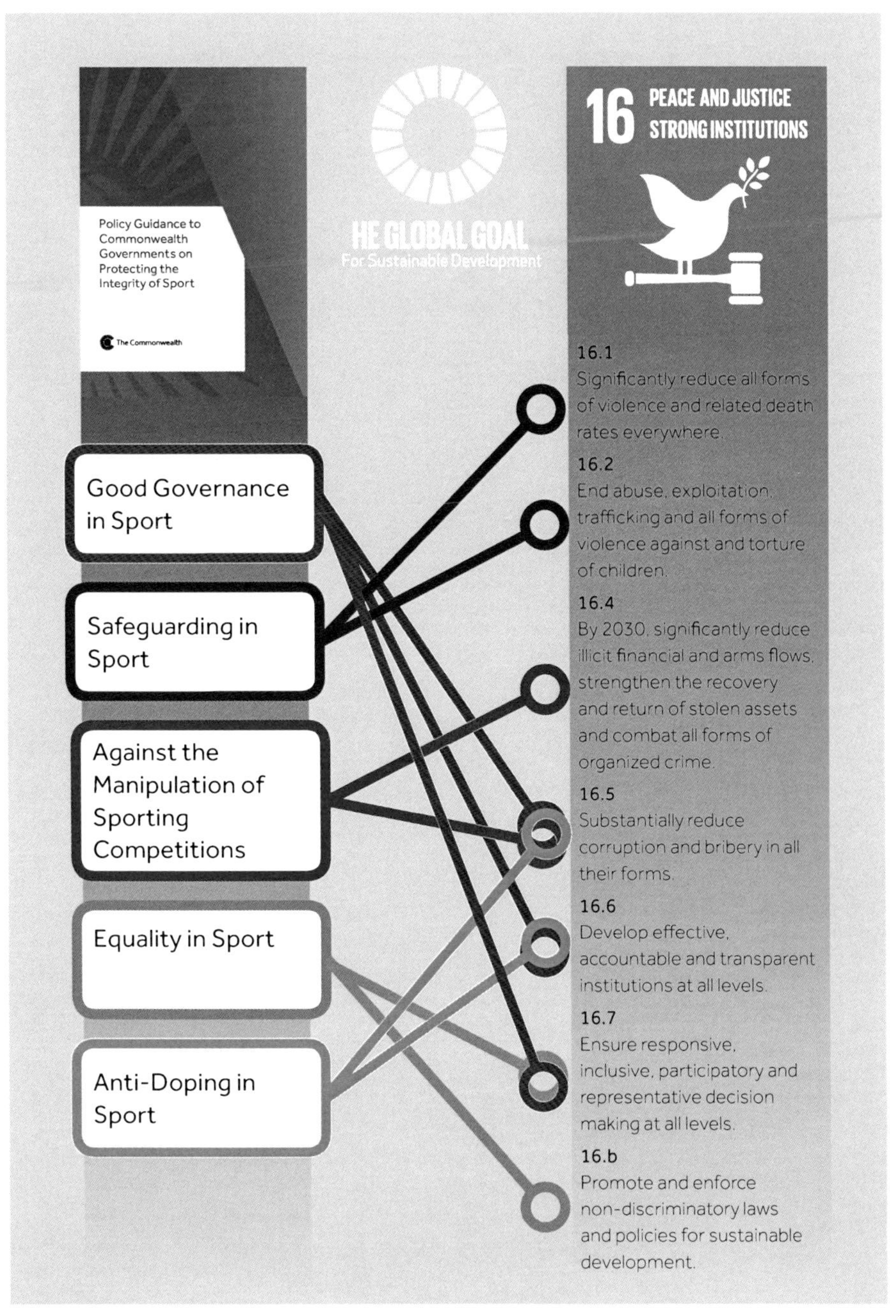

Source: Commonwealth Secretariat (2016)

Table 11.1 Policy options to enhance the contribution of sport to SDG 16

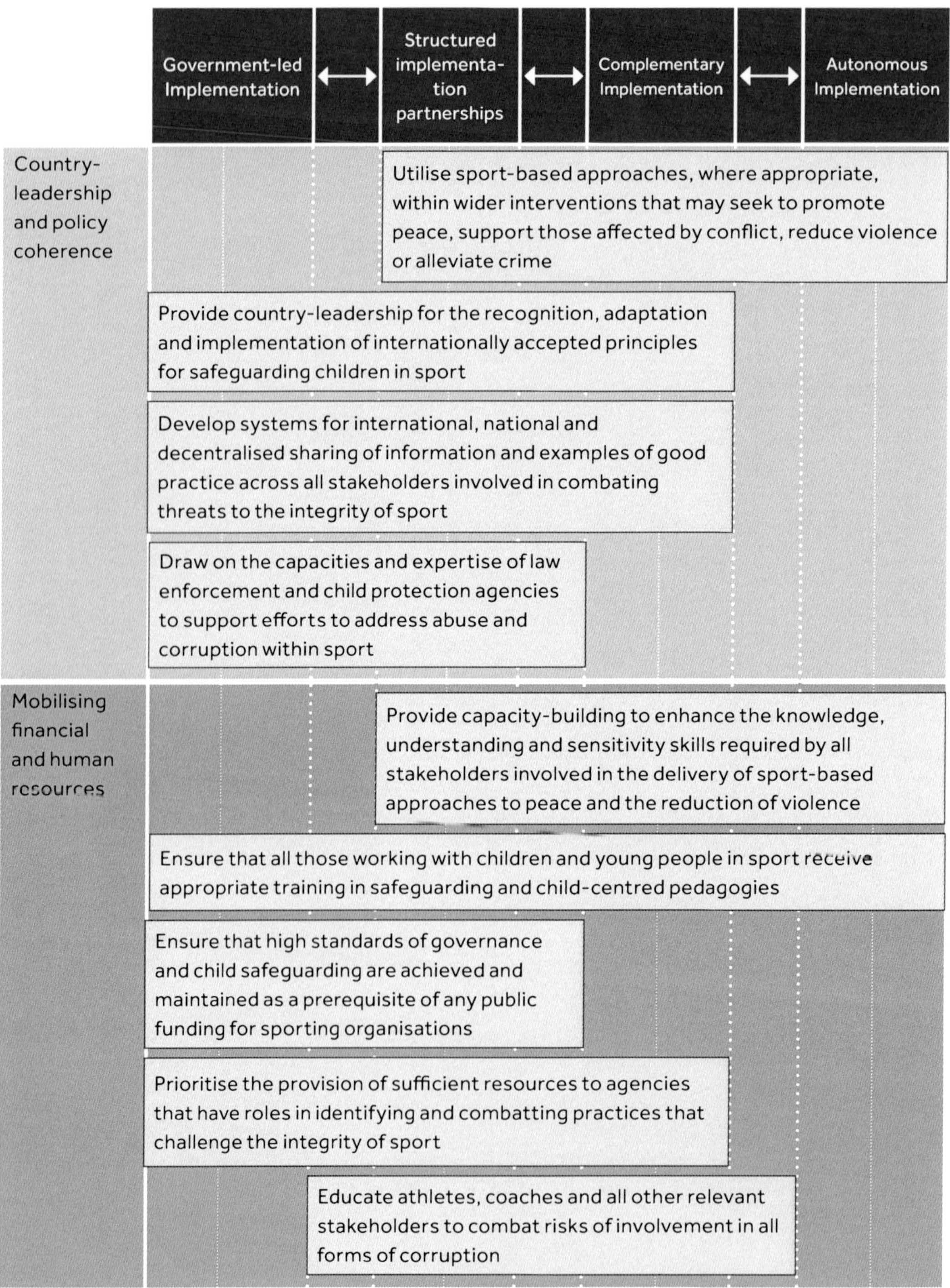

<table>
<tr><th></th><th>Government-led Implementation</th><th>⟷</th><th>Structured implementa-tion partnerships</th><th>⟷</th><th>Complementary Implementation</th><th>⟷</th><th>Autonomous Implementation</th></tr>
<tr><td rowspan="4">Country-leadership and policy coherence</td><td></td><td></td><td colspan="5">Utilise sport-based approaches, where appropriate, within wider interventions that may seek to promote peace, support those affected by conflict, reduce violence or alleviate crime</td></tr>
<tr><td colspan="5">Provide country-leadership for the recognition, adaptation and implementation of internationally accepted principles for safeguarding children in sport</td><td></td><td></td></tr>
<tr><td colspan="5">Develop systems for international, national and decentralised sharing of information and examples of good practice across all stakeholders involved in combating threats to the integrity of sport</td><td></td><td></td></tr>
<tr><td colspan="4">Draw on the capacities and expertise of law enforcement and child protection agencies to support efforts to address abuse and corruption within sport</td><td></td><td></td><td></td></tr>
<tr><td rowspan="5">Mobilising financial and human resources</td><td></td><td></td><td colspan="5">Provide capacity-building to enhance the knowledge, understanding and sensitivity skills required by all stakeholders involved in the delivery of sport-based approaches to peace and the reduction of violence</td></tr>
<tr><td colspan="7">Ensure that all those working with children and young people in sport receive appropriate training in safeguarding and child-centred pedagogies</td></tr>
<tr><td colspan="4">Ensure that high standards of governance and child safeguarding are achieved and maintained as a prerequisite of any public funding for sporting organisations</td><td></td><td></td><td></td></tr>
<tr><td colspan="5">Prioritise the provision of sufficient resources to agencies that have roles in identifying and combatting practices that challenge the integrity of sport</td><td></td><td></td></tr>
<tr><td></td><td colspan="5">Educate athletes, coaches and all other relevant stakeholders to combat risks of involvement in all forms of corruption</td><td></td></tr>
</table>

(*Continued*)

Table 11.1 Policy options to enhance the contribution of sport to SDG 16 (*cont.*)

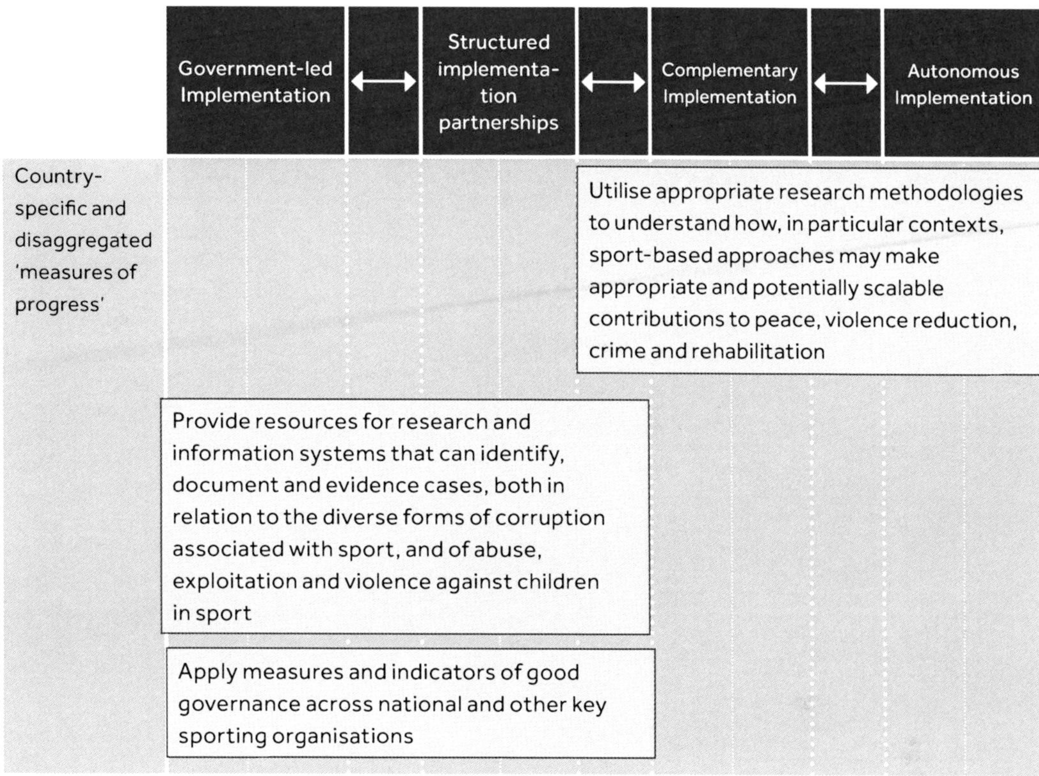

	Government-led Implementation ⟷	Structured implementation partnerships ⟷	Complementary Implementation ⟷	Autonomous Implementation
Country-specific and disaggregated 'measures of progress'			Utilise appropriate research methodologies to understand how, in particular contexts, sport-based approaches may make appropriate and potentially scalable contributions to peace, violence reduction, crime and rehabilitation	
	Provide resources for research and information systems that can identify, document and evidence cases, both in relation to the diverse forms of corruption associated with sport, and of abuse, exploitation and violence against children in sport			
	Apply measures and indicators of good governance across national and other key sporting organisations			

Note

1 See, for example, Alexander, K., A. Stafford and R. Lewis (2011), *The Experiences of Children Participating in Organized Sport in the UK*, NSPCC, London Brackenridge, C. H., T. Kay and D. J. A. Rhind (Eds) (2012) *Sport, Children's Rights and Violence Prevention: A Source Book on Global Issues and Local Programmes*, Brunel University Press, London; Kirby, S., L. Greaves, and O. Hankivsky (2000), *The Dome of Silence: Sexual Harassment and Abuse in Sport*, Fernwood Publishing, Halifax; Leahy, T., G. Pretty and G. Tenenbaum (2002), 'Prevalence of sexual Abuse in organized competitive Sport in Australia', *Journal of Sexual Aggression*, Vol. 8: 16–36; and Rhind, D. J. A., J. McDermott, E. Lambert and I. Koleva (2014), 'Managing safeguarding cases in sport', *Child Abuse Review*, Vol. 23.

References

Alm, J. (Ed.) (n.d.), *Action for Good Governance in International Sports Organisations*, available at: http://www.playthegame.org/fileadmin/documents/Good_governance_reports/Final_AGGIS_leaflet.pdf

Burleson, C. (2012), 'The ancient Olympic truce in modern-day peacekeeping: revisiting Ekecheiria', *Sport in Society*, Vol. 15, 798–813.

Chappelet, J.-L. and M. Mrkonjic (2013), *Basic Indicators for Better Governance in International Sport (Bibgis): An Assessment Tool for International Sport Governing Bodies*, available at: http://www.idheap.ch/idheap.nsf/view/D6156F1EF87ACB07C1257B3900538D87/$File/IDHEAP%20Working%20Paper#x0025;p201-2013.pdf

Coalter, F. (2013), '"There is loads of relationships here": developing a programme theory for sport-for-change programmes', *International Review for the Sociology of Sport*, Vol. 48, 594–612.

Commonwealth Advisory Body on Sport (CABOS) (2015), *Draft Principles for a Framework of Commonwealth Consensus on Integrity in Sport*, discussion paper presented to the Commonwealth Advisory Body on Sport Meeting, June 2015.

Commonwealth Secretariat (2013), The Charter of the *Commonwealth*, available at: www.thecommonwealth.org/our-charter

Commonwealth Secretariat (2016), *Policy Guidance to Commonwealth Governments on Protecting the Integrity of Sport*, available at: http://thecommonwealth.org/sites/default/files/inline/Policy%20Guidance%20to%20Commonwealth%20Governments%20on%20Protecting%20the%20Integrity%20of%20Sport%202016.pdf

Ha, J. P. and A. Lyras (2013), 'Sport for refugee youth in a new society: the role of acculturation in sport for development and peace programming', *South African Journal for Research in Sport, Physical Education and Recreation*, Vol. 35, 121–140.

Hanstad, D. V. and B. Houlihan (2015), 'Strengthening global anti-doping policy through bilateral collaboration: the example of Norway and China', *International Journal of Sport Policy and Politics*, Vol. 7, 587–604.

Houlihan, B. and R. Giulianotti (2012), 'Politics and the London 2012 Olympics: the (in) security Games', *International Affairs*, Vol. 88, 701–717.

International Olympic Committee (IOC) (2008), *Basic Universal Principles of Good Governance of the Olympic and Sports Movement*, available at: http://www.olympic.org/Documents/Conferences_Forums_and_Events/2008_seminar_autonomy/Basic_Universal_Principles_of_Good_Governance.pdf

International Safeguarding Children in Sport Working Group (2014), *International Safeguards for Children in Sport*, available at: http://www.unicef.org.uk/Documents/Sport-documents/International%20Safeguards%20for%20Children%20in%20Sport%20FINAL_updated%20 2016.pdf

Lang, M. and M. Hartill (2014), *Safeguarding, Child Protection and Abuse in Sport: International perspectives in research, policy and practice*, Routledge, Abingdon.

Nichols, G. (2010), *Sport and Crime Reduction: The Role of Sports in Tackling Youth Crime*, Routledge, Abingdon.

Rhind, D., C. Brackenridge, T. Kay and F. Owusu-Sekyere (2016), 'Child protection and SDP: the post-MDG agenda for policy, practice and research', in Hayhurst, L. M. C., T. Kay and M. Chawansky (Eds), *Beyond Sport for Development and Peace: Transnational Perspectives on Theory, Policy and Practice*, Routledge, Abingdon, 72–86.

Schulenkorf, N. (2010), 'The roles and responsibilities of a change agent in sport event development projects', *Sport Management Review*, Vol. 13, 118–128.

Sen, A. (Ed.) (2011), *Peace and Democratic Society*, Open Book Publishers/Commonwealth Secretariat, London.

Sugden, J. (2010), 'Critical left-realism and sport interventions in divided societies', *International Review for the Sociology of Sport*, Vol. 45, 258–272.

Transparency International (2015), *Global Corruption Report: Sport*, available at: http://www.transparency.org/news/feature/sport_integrity#articles

Twyford, L. (2016), 'The post-MDG agenda for policy, practice and research: Making sport safer for children everywhere', in Hayhurst, L. M. C., T. Kay and M. Chawansky (Eds), *Beyond Sport for Development and Peace: Transnational Perspectives on Theory, Policy and Practice*, Routledge, Abingdon, 87–93.

United Nations General Assembly (UNGA) (2015), *Transforming our World: The 2030 Agenda for Sustainable Development*, available at: www.un.org/ga/search/view_doc.asp?symbol=A/70/L.1andLang=E

UNESCO (2005), *International Convention Against Doping in Sport*, available at: http://unesdoc.unesco.org/images/0014/001425/142594m.pdf#page=2

UNESCO (2013), *Declaration of Berlin*, available at: http://unesdoc.unesco.org/images/0022/002211/221114e.pdf

UNICEF (2010), *Protecting Children from Violence in Sport*, available at: http://www.unicef-irc.org/publications/pdf/violence_in_sport.pdf

UNICEF (2014), *Hidden in Plain Sight: A statistical analysis of violence against children*, available at: http://www.unicef.org/publications/index_74865.html#

United Nations (1989), *The United Nations Convention on the Rights of the Child*, available at: http://www.unicef.org.uk/Documents/Publication-pdfs/UNCRC_PRESS200910web.pdf.

UNOSDP (2010), *Sport and Child and Youth Development: Thematic Working Group*, available at: http://www.un.org/wcm/webdav/site/sport/shared/sport/pdfs/SDP%20IWG/Action%20Plan_Sport%20and%20Child%20%26%20Youth%20Development_FINAL_New.pdf

Wilson, B., N. Van Luijk and M. K. Boit (2015), 'When celebrity athletes are "social movement entrepreneurs": A study of the role of elite runners in run-for-peace events in post-conflict Kenya in 2008', *International Review for the Sociology of Sport*, 50(8), 929–957.

Appendix

Consultation

The following experts were consulted through the process of producing this guide:

Anna Barrett	Partners of America
Bella Bello Bitugu	University of Ghana
Adele Catzim-Sanchez	Ministry of Education, Youth Sport and Culture, Government of Belize
Bessie Chelemu	Ministry of Youth, Sport and Child Development, Government of Zambia
Derek Bardowell	Laureus Sport for Good Foundation
Paul Darby	University of Ulster
Caroline Dodd-Reynolds	Durham University
Ruth Jeanes	Monash University
Tess Kay	Brunel University
Selina Khoo	University of Malaya/CABOS
Melanie Lang	Edge Hill University
Jackie Lauff	Sport Matters
Robert Morini	UK Sport
Lorraine Nicholas	Organisation of Eastern Caribbean States
Emily Oliver	Durham University
Ben Sanders	Grassroot Soccer
Nico Schulenkorf	University of Technology Sydney
Emma Sherry	La Trobe University
Alan Thomson	Edge Hill University
Liz Twyford	UNICEF UK
Oliver Dudfield	Commonwealth Secretariat
Malcolm Dingwall-Smith	Commonwealth Secretariat
Tikwiza Silubonde	Commonwealth Secretariat

Commonwealth Advisory Body on Sport

Seth Osei Agyen	Ministry of Youth and Sports, Ghana
Hilary Beckles	University of the West Indies
Max Fuzani	Ministry of Sport and Recreation, South Africa
Jacqueline Gertze	Namibia Football Association

(Continued)

Andrew Godkin	Office of Sport, Department of Health, Australia
Dian Gomes	Nominee of Ministry of Tourism and Sports, Sri Lanka
David Grevemberg	Commonwealth Games Federation
Assmaah Helal	Commonwealth Youth Sport for Development and Peace Working Group
Selina Khoo	University of Malay
Louise Martin (Chair)	sportscotland; nominee of Department of Culture, Media and Sport, Government of the United Kingdom
Mark Mungal	Caribbean Sport and Development Agency
Al-Hassan Yakmut	National Sports Council of Nigeria

The following organisations and institutions participated in the Commonwealth's consultation on sport and the SDGs:

Commonwealth Sport and Post-2015 Expert Roundtable – London, United Kingdom, April, 2015

Agitos Foundation, International Paralympic Committee

Commonwealth Games Federation

Commonwealth Youth Sport for Development and Peace Working Group

Department for Culture, Media and Sport, Government of the United Kingdom

Durham University

Fight for Peace

International Inspiration

Laureus Sport for Good Foundation

Loughborough University

Nike, Inc.

UK Sport

UNICEF UK

Wheeling Happiness Foundation

CABOS regional consultation on sport and the post-2015 development agenda – Port of Spain, Trinidad and Tobago, June 2015

Caribbean Sport and Development Agency

Commonwealth Games Federation

Commonwealth Youth Sport for Development and Peace Working Group

International Centre for Sport Security

Ministry of Youth and Sports, Government of Ghana

Ministry of Youth and Sport, Government of Saint Kitts and Nevis

Namibia Football Association

National Sports Council of Nigeria

Office of Sport, Department of Health, Government of Australia

Organisation of East Caribbean States

Special Olympics

sportscotland

University of Malay

UNICEF Namibia

University of West Indies

Commonwealth Sport and Post-2015 Forum – London, United Kingdom, June 2015

Audacious Dreams Foundation

The Change Foundation

Comic Relief

Commonwealth Games Federation

Commonwealth Youth Sport for Development and Peace Working Group

Department for Culture Media and Sport, Government of the United Kingdom

Durham University

Fight for Peace

German Federal Enterprise for International Cooperation (GIZ)

High Commission for Saint Lucia in London

Interdisciplinary Centre for Sports Science and Development, University of Western Cape

International Centre for Sport Security – Enterprise

International Centre for Sport Security – Europe

International Inspiration

International Netball Federation

Laureus Sport for Good Foundation

Loughborough University

Magic Bus

Ministry of Education, Sport and Culture, Government of Samoa

Ministry of Sports and Culture, Government of Rwanda

Ministry of Tourism and Sports, Government of Sri Lanka

Ministry of Youth and Sports, Government of Ghana

Peace and Sport

Right to Play

Sportanddev.org

Sport in Action

sportscotland

UNESCO

UNICEF

UK Sport

Women Win

Youth Sport Trust

Expert Roundtable on 'the Contribution of Sport to the Post-2015 Development Agenda' – Lusaka, Zambia, July 2015

International Inspiration

Ministry of Youth and Sport, Government of Zambia

National Olympic Committee of Zambia

National Paralympic Committee for Zambia

National Sports Council of Zambia

Olympic Youth Development Centre

Sport in Action

University of Zambia

Commonwealth Senior Officials Meeting on Sport for Development and Peace – Apia, Samoa, September 2015

Department of Home Affairs, Government of Nauru

Department of Sports, Government of Nauru

Government of Tokelau

Ministry of Education, Youth and Sports, Government of Tuvalu

Ministry of Internal Affairs, Government of Tonga

Ministry of Women, Community and Social Development (MWCSD), Government of Samoa

Ministry of Women, Youth, Children and Family Affairs, Government of the Solomon Islands

Ministry for Youth and Sports Development, Government of Vanuatu

Ministry of Youth and Sports, Government of Fiji

National Youth Council of Fiji

Secretariat of Pacific Community

UNICEF Pacific

Commonwealth Expert Roundtable on Evaluating the Contribution of Sport to Sustainable Development – London, United Kingdom, April 2016

Laureus Sport for Good Foundation

Department for International Development, Government of the United Kingdom

Partners of the Americas

Commonwealth Youth Sport for Development & Peace Working Group

University of Ghana

Ministry of Education, Youth, Sport & Culture, Government of Belize

Ministry of Youth & Sport, Government of Zambia

Special Olympics

Leeds Beckett University

Swiss Academy for Development

sportanddev.org

International Inspiration

InFocus

University of Malaya

Sport Matters

Durham University

Overseas Development Institute

UNESCO

Organisation of Eastern Caribbean States

Office of Sport, Government of Australia

Youth Sport Trust

Grassroot Soccer

International Working Group on Women and Sport

UNICEF

World Health Organization